CHILD'S PLAY:
FACILITATING PLAY ON HOUSING ESTATES

ROB WHEWAY AND ALISON MILLWARD

A REPORT FOR THE CHARTERED INSTITUTE OF HOUSING
AND THE JOSEPH ROWNTREE FOUNDATION

The Chartered Institute of Housing
The Chartered Institute of Housing is the professional organisation for all people who work in housing. Its purpose is to take a strategic and leading role in encouraging and promoting the provision of good quality affordable housing for all. The Institute has more than 13,000 members working in local authorities, housing associations, the private sector and educational institutions.

Chartered Institute of Housing
Octavia House, Westwood Way
Coventry CV4 8JP
Telephone: 01203 694433

The Joseph Rowntree Foundation
The Joseph Rowntree Foundation has supported this project as part of its programme of research and innovative development projects, which it hopes will be of value to policy makers and practitioners. The facts presented and views expressed in this report, however, are those of the authors and not necessarily those of the Foundation.

Joseph Rowntree Foundation
The Homestead
40 Water End
York YO3 6LP
Telephone: 01904 629241

Child's Play: Facilitating Play on Housing Estates
Written by Rob Wheway and Alison Millward

© Rob Wheway and Alison Millward 1997
Published by the Chartered Institute of Housing
ISBN 0 9000396 26 2

Graphic design by Jeremy Spencer
Cover illustration by Ant Parker
Printed by Hobbs, Totton, Southampton

Whilst all reasonable care and attention has been taken in compiling this publication, the authors and the publishers regret that they cannot assume responsibility for any error or omission that it contains.

All rights reserved. No part of this publication may be reproduced, stored in a retrieval system or transmitted in any form or by any means, electronic, mechanical, photocopying, recording, or otherwise without the prior permission of the publishers.

Contents

Acknowledgments	v
About the authors	vi
Executive summary	1
Introduction	**8**
The context	8
The children's voice	9
Opportunity and choice	10
Play patterns	12
Range	13
Ethnicity	15
Mobility	15
Estate design	18
The provision of play space	21
The promotion and supervision of play	23
Play fashions	24
Involvement	25
Research approach	**27**
Aims of the research	27
Research methods: observations and interview surveys	28
Involving children and young people in the process of change	30
Planning and development issues	30
Findings	**32**
Location	32
Basic activity	36
Key activity	37
The proportion of children outdoors	38
Age group and gender differences	39
Favourite places to play	40
Parental perceptions	44
Suggested improvements	44
Layout	45
Supervised play	46

Summary of findings on each estate	49
Conclusions	51

Whose estate is it anyway? Involving young clients in the planning and design process 53

Guidelines 60

Checklist for planners and estate managers 63
Supervision 66
Crime and safety considerations 66

Appendix: JRF – Observation coding system 69

Bibliography 71

ACKNOWLEDGEMENTS

Alison Millward and Rob Wheway, the principal researchers on the study, would like to thank all the members of the advisory group and Julie Brewerton at JRF for their enthusiastic and valuable support, and Mike, Parminder, Paddy and Sarah for their help with the field work. Louise Brooke-Smith provided essential planning and development expertise.

Any errors of fact remain entirely the responsibility of the principal researchers.

About the Authors

Alison Millward, PhD, BS(Hons), MIEEM, is an environmental consultant specialising in open space research, community action, nature conservation and landscape planning. Alison Millward Associates, 20 Reddings Road, Moseley, Birmingham, B13 8LN. Tel/fax: 0121 449 9181.

Rob Wheway, MSc, MEd, MILAM MIMgt, is a specialist in children's play with a background in playwork, play policy development, play equipment inspection and sales, and research. Wheway Consultancy, 87 Allesley Old Road, Coventry, CV5 8DB. Tel: 01203 714 784, Fax: 01203 714 530, e-mail: rob@wheway.demon.co.uk

EXECUTIVE SUMMARY

The outdoor environment has long been a favourite place to play for children and there are several publications that provide guidance on the design of school playgrounds, adventure playgrounds and play areas (NPFA, 1992; Coffin and Williams 1989, and Titman, 1994).

However, it is also known that children tend to spend relatively short amounts of time (less than 15 minutes) at play in these formal outdoor environments (Naylor, 1985; Ellis, 1973; Hole, 1966). The majority of time spent outdoors involves children moving around the outdoor environment they have access to and playing *en route* (Moore, 1986). Children appreciate having a diversity of places to play close to home, and their favourite places to play include parks, other open spaces, and play areas (DoE, 1973). Play is the way that children learn about themselves and the world they live in. In the process of mastering familiar situations and learning to cope with new ones, their intelligence and personality grow, as well as their bodies. The environment for play should therefore offer a richness of opportunity, allow each child to exercise choice, and to grow, safely, at their own rate (Dattner, 1969).

Driven by the need to maximise profits, there is and has been throughout the 1980s and 1990s, a genuine reluctance amongst private house builders to formally allocate land for play purposes within estates. Social housing providers often find themselves torn between space for play or high density housing to meet ever pressing housing needs. Nevertheless, through development plan policies and planning gain conditions, developers are increasingly required to set aside land or commute sums, to provide open spaces and play areas. The problem of where to locate play areas is widespread, and often results in play areas being pushed onto land on the edge of estates, away from main thoroughfares and house frontages, which would otherwise afford a level of informal community supervision. Examples of developers having integrated the needs of children (other than to reduce car speeds and provide an amount of informal open space) in the design of the outdoor environment of housing estates, are difficult to find.

Children under 16 years of age account for approximately 20 per cent of the population and on housing association and council housing estates the proportion can rise to 50 per cent. There is evidence to suggest that the distance primary school children are able to travel from home on their own continues to shrink (estimated now, for example, as only 280 metres for nine year old girls) although bike ownership may have doubled in the last 20 years. The quality and diversity of the outdoor environment within two streets of the front door is therefore extremely important if children's needs for active, quiet, imaginative, creative and social play are to be satisfied.

❏ Aims of the Study

The aims of this research were developed to:
- determine where children play outdoors, what they do there and the proportion outdoors at any one time;
- identify favourite places for play and the reasons why they are popular;
- draw out the type of improvements children and parents would like to see made to their estates;
- identify processes by which children and young people can be involved in the planning and design or re-design of housing estates; and
- provide a set of guidelines for planners and providers on children's needs from the outdoor environment on housing estates and how these might translate into estate design and management.

❏ Approach

During the school summer holidays of 1996, over 3,500 observations were made of children (under 18 years of age) at play on 12 housing estates built between the 1890s and 1990s, by housing associations, local authorities and private developers. Observations at each estate, covered six hour long sessions at different times of the day and the children were recorded for their location, basic mode of activity, and key activity.

Following the period of observations, 236 children (between 5 and 18 years of age) and 82 parents were interviewed using a standard questionnaire format.

Information was also gathered from estate managers, local planners and youth workers about their perceptions of where children played on the estates and any problems or particular benefits associated with this.

❑ Findings

Children seek social contact with their friends through their play activity outdoors and to achieve this they need to be able to move around their estate as widely and safely as possible and from an early age (two plus). Roads and pavements remain the most frequently used locations for play (46 per cent of all observations). The reasons for this are partly choice, because this is where the children can most easily meet up with friends in a spontaneous way, and also because a significant amount of play involves moving around the estate (either on foot or by bike) for its own sake, or to call on friends.

Pedestrian and cycling paths are very popular where they exist and help to reduce the proportion of children at play on vehicular roads. This reduces the risk of traffic accidents and extends the range of the children who live on such estates. The ability to walk, run, push a buggy, skate or cycle around the block using a footpath network, without having to cross a road, is greatly valued by children and their parents.

The majority of play outdoors is active (75 per cent) involving walking, running, ball games, use of wheeled vehicles and play equipment. The highest levels of imaginative play were measured on estates with a variety of front street surfaces, front gardens and access to raw materials from nearby informal open space.

The most successful estates, as measured by:
- the widest range of locations available;
- the highest relative safety of the front street;

- the widest range of activities engaged in by the children;
- parental assessment;

were those estates with:

- traffic calming, street closure, walls and driveways;
- grassy areas set back from the roads, a footpath network (for pedestrians and cycles) around and through the estate linking into the public open spaces; and
- culs-de-sac layout with a spinal footpath network, and informal play areas.

The 1990s housing association estates both incorporated play areas in central locations for younger children and a footpath network which enabled a good level of relatively safe mobility for even the youngest children. These estates contain a high proportion of young children and are well designed to meet their needs. Older children are less well provided for, within the immediate curtilage of these estates, although parks, sports pitches and footpath networks were all available in adjacent locations.

The least successful estate was the turn of the century inner city terrace neighbourhood in Coventry. Its traffic calmed counterpart in Birmingham performed somewhat better for play opportunity in the front street. In both cases, the availability of well equipped play areas and sports pitches in nearby parks proved to be critical for all ages.

❑ Processes for involving children and young people

No one method or process for involving children and young people in the planning and design or re-design of housing estates has been identified as consistently successful. A wide variety of methods are being used including planning for real, youth forums, detached youth worker projects, and surveys and presentations.

It is proving difficult for enablers to ensure that children and young people continue their involvement, after the initial consultation phase, during later fundraising, implementation, management and monitoring phases. We have found no examples as yet where the process of involvement could be said to have been comprehensive, integrated with adult led initiatives, or continuing.

As there is currently a strong wave of desire to try to involve young people more in planning issues, as for example through City Challenge and Local Agenda 21 initiatives, there remains a need to evaluate the effectiveness of the different approaches being tried out.

❑ Guidelines and a checklist

From the findings of the study, as amended by consideration of commercial, crime and safety factors, a set of guidelines has been developed for architects, planners, estate managers and others on how the needs of children might best be met.

The ideal estate would be designed so that children would be able to move freely throughout the neighbourhood, able to enjoy a wide variety of social interactions and opportunities for physical, imaginative and creative play.

Guidelines:

Objective	Measure
1. To enable children to move freely round their estate on foot, bicycle, skates, or other wheeled vehicle.	• Footpath network linked to grassy areas, tarmaced areas, play areas, school, shops and bus routes.
2. To travel safely without danger from traffic.	• Traffic calming measures to limit car speeds to 10 mph: short straight sections, bumps, culs-de-sac, change in surface material or colour, roundels, pinch points, mini-roundabouts and sleeping policemen. • Culs-de-sac and no through route layout. • Narrow sight lines on approach roads and sharp angle turns into residential roads. • Wide sight lines to enable drivers to see children moving between pavement and road within residential roads. • Car parking off road, on drives or in bays to increase visibility of children moving between pavement and road.
3. To be able to play in front, or within sight, of their homes.	• A variety of play spaces and surfaces incorporated in the front street landscape, such as walls, sitting areas, grassy areas, and sections of wider pavement, to encourage girls especially to play outdoors, as they tend to have more restrictions placed on them than boys. • Front gardens with good visual oversight from house kitchens and living rooms. • Footpath network linked to grassy areas, tarmaced areas, play areas, school, shops and bus routes.

Objective	Measure
4. To be part of the community and the community's interactions.	<ul><li>A variety of play spaces and surfaces incorporated in the front street landscape, such as walls, sitting areas, grassy areas and sections of wider pavement, to encourage girls especially to play outdoors, as they tend to have more restrictions placed on them than boys.</li><li>Public open spaces located along popular pedestrian routes to shopping centres, schools and other well used public buildings such as estate offices, to increase the level of informal community supervision.</li></ul>
5. To be able to play in the natural environment.	<ul><li>Trees and hedgerows conserved and incorporated as street landscape features to encourage climbing and imaginative play.</li><li>Public open spaces incorporating play equipment (swings and a slide especially), trees, wild areas and flat grassy areas for ball games.</li></ul>
6. To be able to play in purposefully provided play opportunities.	<ul><li>Play areas located along footpath network, within public open space, adjacent to public buildings or well used pedestrian routes, to allow for a level of informal community supervision.</li><li>A variety of play spaces and surfaces incorporated in the front street landscape, such as walls, sitting areas, grassy areas, and sections of wider pavement, to encourage girls especially to play outdoors, as they tend to have more restrictions placed on them than boys.</li></ul>
7. To be able to play football and other ball games.	<ul><li>Public open spaces incorporating play equipment (swings and a slide especially), trees, wild areas and flat grassy areas for ball games.</li><li>For seniors and teenagers, a footpath network, flat surfaces for sporting activity, laid out pitches and courts, a fishing pool and places to meet, in public open spaces, within or adjacent to estates.</li></ul>
8. To be able to play outdoors within the home environment.	<ul><li>Back gardens with sections of fence or gate which allow children to see what is going on in the street.</li><li>Front gardens with good visual oversight from kitchens and living rooms.</li></ul>
9. To be able to attend playschemes, clubs or other organised activities.	<ul><li>Facilities designed or useable for playwork, either paid or voluntary, regular or occasional.</li><li>Play areas located along footpath network, within public open space, adjacent to public buildings or well used pedestrian routes, to allow for a level of informal community supervision.</li></ul>

Finally, a checklist is provided to help providers assess the quality of provision to meet children's needs from the outdoor environment of housing estates on proposed and existing estates (see pages 63-66).

INTRODUCTION

❑ The context

The outdoor environment has long been a favourite place to play for children, but it is also known that children tend to spend relatively short amounts of time at play in formal outdoor environments such as play areas, adventure playgrounds and school playgrounds (Coffin and Williams, 1989). The majority of children's play outdoors takes place near the home and in moving around the outdoor environment they have access to, playing *en route* (Moore, 1986).

The Joseph Rowntree Foundation, itself a provider of housing through its role as a housing association, wanted to build on current knowledge and expertise in facilitating play on housing estates, examine areas of good practice, and bring together a set of clear authoritative guidelines for planners and providers.

The Foundation wanted these guidelines to include the views of all the key players including the often forgotten children, teenagers and their parents.

There is a wide range of issues affecting children's use of the outdoor environment for play in the 1990s including:
- the Children Act (1989);
- UN Convention on the Rights of the Child (1989);
- traffic and 'stranger danger';
- lack of funding for maintenance and new provision;
- the rising importance of planning consents to facilitate provision;

- the draw of indoor leisure pursuits; and
- the often conflicting interests of the users, providers and supervisors of children's play facilities.

Children have every right to use the communal areas of estates on which they live for play, and for their needs to be considered in the design process:

Article 31
The right of children to leisure, play and participation in cultural and artistic activities.

Article 24
The child's right to enjoy the highest level of health possible.

Article 15
The right of children to meet with others and to join or set up associations, unless doing so violates the rights of others.

Article 13
The child's right to obtain and make known information, and to express his/her views unless this would violate the rights of others.

UN Convention on the Rights of the Child

The need to achieve sustainable development and to recognise that the solution to many environmental problems lies in recognising the links between social, economic and environmental problems is also relevant to this research. It is widely hoped that by encouraging all sectors of society and particularly children, to define the kind of environments they want to live in, for example through Local Agenda 21 action plans, such involvement will help to bring about change, and sustainable change, for the better.

❑ The children's voice

A number of recent good practice guides have been produced including the revised NPFA *The Six Acre Standard* (NPFA 1992), which provides guidelines for neighbourhood and local areas for play; *Children's outdoor play in the built environment: a handbook for all who design, plan or manage residential neighbourhoods*, which makes particular reference to the needs of children with disabilities (Coffin and Williams, 1989); and *Special Places; Special People*, a critique of "the hidden agenda of school grounds" which examines the way in which the environment of school grounds affects children's attitudes and behaviour (Titman, 1994). Like so many researchers, Titman found that whilst there was a good deal of research that concerned children and their relationship with the outdoor environment, very little of it had involved children. And, such involvement with children as had happened, had been so resource intensive that it was unlikely to be widely replicated.

Public participation, tenant participation and community involvement have become watchwords in the regeneration of old housing estates throughout the 1980s and 1990s. Such involvement is seen as essential to achieving a successful outcome from the design process and yet the examples where children have been involved would seem to be rare.

❑ Opportunity and choice

Outdoor play is popular at all ages, and includes physical, imaginative, creative, social, solitary and intellectual activities. Children can be found outdoors at play any time in the pre-school years, and when older, before and after school, at weekends and in the school holidays. Only half the days in the year are school days and even on school days there is still significant time available for play outdoors.

As children grow older they are able to range further from home sometimes with or without permission. It is known that children value outdoor environments where there are lots of things to do (Akehurst and Wheway, 1982), and which provide for their psychological as well as physical needs (DoE, 1973). The outdoor environment remains the preferred place to play though not necessarily the most used place (DoE, 1973 and Moore, 1986). Access and diversity are the recurrent themes of many studies which have sought to examine how children play outdoors and what they prefer. The outdoor environment is believed to offer children a continual source of novelty for exploration, contact with living things, a source of raw materials for creative and constructive play and greater opportunities for meeting new children and adults than is possible within the home or school (Moore and Young, 1978; Naylor, 1985). Children can also impart rich meanings to landscape features and experience strong emotional responses to it (Titman,

1994; Rhode and Kendle, 1994). The elements of nature such as bushes, rocks, trees and sand, dominate the reasons adults give for liking remembered outdoor places from childhood, and the places best remembered tend to be those experienced between the ages of four and ten.

The indoor alternatives to a bad outdoor play environment are, today, so stimulating and powerful (television and computer games) that it is possible to find open spaces where children constitute a very low percentage of the users. However, there are others where children and teenagers account for 30-60 per cent of all the users (Millward and Mostyn, 1988), an open space with that kind of pull on children must have something of value to them. So it may prove to be with certain housing estates. Whether by design or default, those with the highest percentages of children observed at play might in some way be considered good by the children and perhaps relatively safe by their parents. The relative availability and range of opportunities for play that children have access to, and the degree to which they can control their own play activities, have been found to have a direct bearing on the type of adult they become (Piaget, 1951; McLellan, 1968; Holme and Massie, 1970; Dattner, 1969).

In repeat studies, rural children from Humberside (Akehurst and Wheway, 1982), and urban children from Birmingham (Millward, 1989), preferred play places that offered "lots of things to do". Grass was valued especially for ball games and also just to sit on. Many of the children expressed their appreciation of the peacefulness and privacy of their play places. Natural areas were mentioned by over 50 per cent of the rural children in the Humberside Study as places they liked to play in contrast to only 14 per cent of the Birmingham children.

When asked to describe what they considered the **ideal** place to play, the Birmingham children mentioned parks, playgrounds (particularly adventure playgrounds with assault courses), gardens with flowers, grassy fields and 'proper' sports pitches (for girls and boys) most frequently. The range of other places mentioned was very wide and included natural areas (nature reserves, dumps to make dens in and ponds), zoos, islands, "a place in the clouds", Disneyland, and many indoor places such as play centres, swimming baths, roller rinks, youth clubs and museums.

Of the elements of these places, equipment was of key importance. In decreasing order of popularity, swings, slides, climbing frames, roundabouts, see-saws and assault courses were most popular (which is exactly the order given in the Humberside Study, except that roundabouts and see-saws were reversed).

Interestingly, the children mentioned several social factors that contributed to the value of their ideal places. The boys and girls were equally concerned that there should be provision for little children as well as older ones. Others wanted people there to stop vandalism and to hire bikes from, they wanted to feel safe, away from roads and undisturbed. They also wanted their play places to be free from dogs and broken glass, and one wit suggested that there should be more signs permitting (rather than prohibiting) ball games.

❑ Play patterns

In the last major study of play on housing estates (DoE, 1973), over 75 per cent of the children observed outdoors were playing near their homes and most of this was on roads, pavements and paved areas. The children were mainly engaged in physical activities such as walking and running, using wheeled vehicles, play equipment and ball games. Just over a quarter of the play observed involved sitting, standing or some other sedentary activity and never more than 20 per cent of children were observed to be outdoors at any one time. Half the children cited parks, and places with swings, slides and space for playing ball games as their favourite places, and just under a third mentioned play areas. The majority of the parents interviewed in this study thought there were not enough play facilities in their areas, even on the estates where they were provided and the researchers concluded that the call for more play facilities was being used as a catch-all for a wider range of concerns parents had about bringing their children up.

The consideration of outdoor playing space as such, is not regarded by central government as a strategic planning matter. There are no statutory limits for the minimum amount of outdoor playing space that children must have access to, be it formal or informal, within or without housing development areas. Planning Policy Guidance Note 17 (PPG17) requires local planning authorities to take account of the community's needs for recreational space, to resist pressures for its development, and identify deficiencies in provision. PPG17 suggests that local authorities draw up their own standards for provision and that these could be modelled on those set down in *The Six Acre Standard* of the National Playing Fields Association

(NPFA, 1992). Any such standard should reflect ease of access, particularly on foot.

> Such provision is essential because children play outdoors on a regular daily basis, close to home and without formal leadership.
> NPFA, *The Six Acre Standard*. 1992, p 38.

The NPFA standard of 6 acres or 2.4 hectares outdoor playing space per 1000 head of population includes provision for 0.4-0.5 hectares of 'casual' or 'informal' playspace within housing areas but specifically excludes woodlands and surface water areas because of:

> a lack of ready accessibility within normal walking time from home [to these types of open space].

Yet the NPFA acknowledges that children often prefer informal and unsafe playing space and for the older child and teenager it is the space (rather than equipment) and the opportunity for socialising that become the most important factors in provision.

❑ Range

In a new departure from previous practice, the NPFA standard now also reflects a time based criterion for measuring provision of outdoor playing space within housing areas (see Appendix H, NPFA, 1992). Young children, of all abilities, up to the age of eight and accompanied by an adult, are expected to travel 100 metres or for one minute to an informal Local Area for Play (LAP) and for five minutes or 400 metres to a Local Equipped Play Area (LEAP).

Whilst the research shows that there are definable limits beyond which children do not travel at every age, there is a counter philosophy put forward that recognises that children do not discriminate strongly between the places they use for play or are obliged to use for play. They interact with the whole neighbourhood and it is the relative diversity of environments within the neighbourhood and the available access to them that are the most important factors for child development (Bjorkild-Chu, 1977; Parkinson, 1985; and van Andel, 1990).

Research shows that there is very little difference in the home range of children, of whatever sex, up until the age of seven (Moore and Young, 1978;

Matthews, 1987). After that there can be a ten-fold increase in home range area with a concomitant increase in path length travelled (Anderson and Tindal, 1972 and Matthews, 1987). Bike owning children from around the age of nine and suburban children of whatever age tend to have a greater home range. Urban children tend to visit more places (Anderson and Tindal, 1972), especially those living in the older parts of cities where there can be more environmental diversity than in new towns or re-developed inner city areas (Moore, 1986). The explanations put forward for this are that play opportunities may be more sparsely distributed around suburban areas and that suburban gardens and backyards may be more sufficient play spaces than those around urban homes.

In his study of 166 children between the ages of 6 and 11 from a suburban school in Coventry, Matthews (1987) confirms the findings of the major US studies on range. He adopted Hart's range typology of free range, range with permission, and range with permission and accompanied by older children. The data in Table 1 shows how the home range (in metres) of boys, begins to extend significantly beyond that of girls from around about the age of 8 until it reaches a peak difference of 40 per cent more at age 11.

Table 1: Home range (metres) for different age groups of suburban children

Age	6 Boy/Girl	7 Boy/Girl	8 Boy/Girl	9 Boy/Girl	10 Boy/Girl	11 Boy/Girl
Free range	<100/<100	189/190	305/199	795/283	967/600	1083/649
Range with permission	210/228	345/320	389/257	915/360	900/597	1136/662
Range when accompanied	290/285	391/364	461/391	963/664	1021/691	1132/745

After Matthews, 1987, gender, home range and environmental cognition.

The main influence on the restriction of girls' ranges would seem to come from parental control. Girls are expected to undertake mothering duties of younger siblings and the parental fear of their daughters becoming the victims of abduction or abuse restricts their range even further. The implication of this must be that girls are likely to be less physically and mentally competent in dealing with the elements of the outdoor environment than boys. The irony of these findings from observational studies is that in perception studies (Millward, 1989 and Moore, 1978) there is very little difference in the number and range of places mentioned by girls and boys.

Teenagers of both sexes, but boys in particular, show an interest in more challenging open spaces including woods, rivers, countryside and beaches (Owens, 1988 and Parkinson, 1985). Conversely there is also a need to seek out places which evoke a sense of security (Bernaldez et al., 1985). Teenagers tend to spend more time in school and tend to use parks (Jendrek, 1988) rather than housing estates for play (Bjorkild-Chu, 1977). Swimming pools and visits to other activity-oriented places are also popular (Parkinson, 1985).

❏ Ethnicity

Few studies have been carried out on the effects of ethnicity on range behaviour. Those that have been attempted have often yielded insufficient cases from which conclusions can be drawn (Parkinson, 1985). Matthews (1992) postulates that children from minority ethnic groups within the UK, may have more restricted ranges than other children because their families tend to concentrate in inner city localities, in poorer housing, and be at the lower end of the income range. Millward (1989) found that the inner city children in her study, many of them Asian, were more heavily restricted by parental control and the fear of harassment, than children from the suburbs.

❏ Mobility

In the last 20 years, the number of cars has risen by 80 per cent and the car has invaded and now dominates the local places where children could once play relatively safely with their friends and within earshot of home (Hillman, 1988). More children are now taken to school by car. The National Travel Survey (Department of Transport, 1995) found that nearly 20 per cent of car driver journeys between 8.30 and 9.00 a.m. were for "escort educational purposes".

Bike riding has also become more dangerous and it could be argued that children's mobility has been reduced because of this at least in relation to their free range behaviour. Conversely, many more parents, but not all, have access to a car and so can take their children further afield to places including the countryside where they can also have contact with the natural world.

The restrictions placed on children are already having a measurable detrimental effect on their physical health. Traffic is forcing parents to restrict their ranges:

> *The 'personal freedom and choice' permitted a typical seven year old in 1971 are now not permitted until children reach the age of about nine and a half.*
> Hillman et al., PSI, 1990.

This lack of activity is resulting in low levels of fitness identified in research by the Sports Council and many other bodies (Allied Dunbar National Fitness Survey, 1992; Cale and Almond, 1992; Armstrong and McManus, 1994; Sleap and Warburton, 1993). One survey noted that:

> *Many of today's children lack stamina; are short of breath after the simplest of exercise; have poor posture leading to lower back pain; are not interested in exercise or sport; are tired and lethargic ... and seem reluctant to walk anywhere.*
> Chartered Society of Physiotherapy, 1995.

As has been widely noted, because cardiovascular risk factors, including obesity, and unfavourable lipid profiles, tend to track from childhood to adulthood, establishing physical activity patterns in childhood is a key to reducing adult cardiovascular diseases (Kuhl and Cooper, 1992; Raitakari et al., 1994; and Harsha, 1995).

It is likely, though not proven, that this decrease in mobility is also having a detrimental effect on their social, creative and imaginative health too. Beyond physical activity, the development of sensory, motoric, emotional and cognitive skills takes place most fully through play. And, independent mobility is important in promoting self-esteem, a strong sense of identity, creative use of one's own mind and the capacity to take responsibility for oneself (Kegerreis, 1993 and Noschis, 1992).

In combining the findings on range and decreased mobility, Wheway (1995) has shown that for a given reduction in range, the overall environment accessible to the child reduces by the square of that reduction. If the range of the nine year old child of today is only the equivalent of the six year old in 1970, the nine year old's accessible environment has reduced to as little as a ninth of what they would have had access to in 1970. Equally, as girls are only allowed half to a third the range of boys, then their accessible environment will be reduced from a quarter to a ninth. Confirmation of this phenomenon comes from Hillman's finding that in 1971, 80 per cent of seven and eight year old children were allowed to go to school without adult supervision. By 1990 this figure had fallen to 9 per cent.

This dramatic decrease in mobility reduces the range of social contact children have with neighbours and therefore may contribute to the dramatic rise in fear of 'stranger danger', which runs contrary to our increasing knowledge that the dangers more often come from a member of the child's own family or a close acquaintance.

The incongruence in the messages being given to children to adopt healthier, more active lifestyles whilst at the same time protecting themselves from traffic, 'stranger danger' and bicycle theft, was investigated by Davis and Jones (1996). They found that 9-10 year olds would prefer to travel to school by bike but were not allowed to do so. Rather than expecting the children to adapt their behaviour these researchers argue that it is within adults' power to modify environments such that they promote, rather than inhibit, children's physical and mental well being. The children in this study also suggested that adults should be setting good examples by cycling, walking and driving more responsibly.

The cycling charity SUSTRAN's recent success in winning £42m of national lottery funds to develop a national cycling network throughout the UK emphasises the growing demand for safe cycle routes around and between settlements, but could not and was not designed to meet the cycling needs of children on individual housing estates.

There do not appear to be any transport figures for the number of walking and cycling journeys made by children in their play time. We believe that it is important for planners and policy makers to understand how large an issue this is.

Based on our observations in this study (reported later in the report) we estimate that an average group of 100 children (typical of the numbers that live on a small housing association estate or in five streets on a council estate or inner city neighbourhood) make somewhere in the region of 281,000 journeys per annum.

Children spend approximately 40 per cent of their play time travelling from one place to another. These places may be relatively close to each other (30-

100 metres) and although the children tend to spend only a few minutes at them, the journeys between them are important for the children. In one hour we therefore estimate that a child might make five journeys.

If we then take a population of 100 children and assume that only half of them play out and for only one hour after school on school days, this generates 250 journeys per day. As school days account for half the days in a year, this generates approximately 45,000 journeys per annum.

If in the same population only 50 per cent play out for an average of two hours on each holiday and weekend day, this generates a further 90,000 journeys per annum.

Finally, if we assume that in addition to all these journeys, each child is likely to make four journeys each day of the year (to school, the shop, a friends, or the ice-cream van, and back again) this generates 146,000 journeys.

Added together this gives us 281,000 journeys per 100 children per annum. Now this may prove to be an over-estimate when tested by further research. On the other hand, having witnessed children at play outside on some estates from 9.00 a.m. until 10.00 p.m. in the summer holidays, it may prove to be a serious underestimate, and the true figure might be nearer 300,000 or even 400,000.

Nonetheless, whether on some estates it is 200,000 or 400,000 journeys per 100 children per annum, these are vast numbers of journeys which are vital for children's freedom to play. They are also journeys which are non-polluting and give healthy exercise.

❑ Estate design

As long ago as the 1960s in *Homes for today and tomorrow* (DoE, 1961), Parker Morris recognised the need to take account of the future dramatic increase in car ownership and how this had to be addressed in the design of housing estates, not just for the benefit of the car owner but also the pedestrian users of estates, and in particular the children:

> *The over-riding concern in designing with the car in mind must be to design for the pedestrian to stay alive. Since in a car-owning community a high proportion of the pedestrians and cyclists will be children, this will demand the segregation of*

pedestrian footpaths and cycleways from road carrying motor vehicles, and preferably the organisation of these footpaths into a system leading from the quiet side of the houses to schools and shops and playspaces, so that children can go about their affairs with reasonable safety. Safety considerations also suggest the importance of arranging for cul-de-sac vehicular approach to residential development, so that vehicles adopt low speeds in the vicinity of homes and so that through traffic does not approach them at all.

Parker Morris also acknowledged that such suggestions were not new as they had long been used in the design of housing areas in the USA under the 'Radburn System'.

Most road accidents in residential areas involve children and 50 per cent of all road accidents to children under five happen within 30 metres of their homes (Karn and Sheridan, 1996).

Design features that can be used to reduce traffic levels and speeds in residential areas include:

- small groups of houses;
- no link from residential roads to main roads;
- short roads (60 metre sections);
- narrow sections of roads and tight bends (small radius 90 degree);
- sleeping policemen;
- shared surface on short roads, with a different surface and a ramp or tight turn to encourage people to drive slowly;
- off street parking and grouped parking spaces; and
- sufficient parking for households and visitors.

Design Bulletin 32 (DoE and DTp, 1992) advocates that changes in the horizontal alignment of roads and shortening of the distance of sections of straight roads are often sufficient to reduce vehicle speeds. For straight lengths of 60 metres, 85 per cent of speeds measured were close to 20 mph which is the speed drivers are requested to travel at within residential areas to prevent fatal accidents to children. Vehicle speeds on even long culs-de-sac and loop roads are lower than those found along other roads with comparable lengths. The use of short culs-de-sac and changes in horizontal alignment cause the least possible discomfort and inconvenience to cyclists, drivers and their passengers and to pedestrians using shared surface roads.

Where further constraints need to be applied, DB32 suggests adopting layouts based on a network configuration (Figure a).

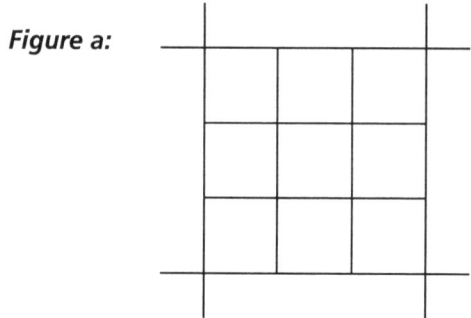

Figure a:

DB 32 also suggests that on estates likely to attract high levels of young families, additional measures can be introduced to exclude non-access traffic using a mixture of loop roads and culs-de-sac (Figures b and c):

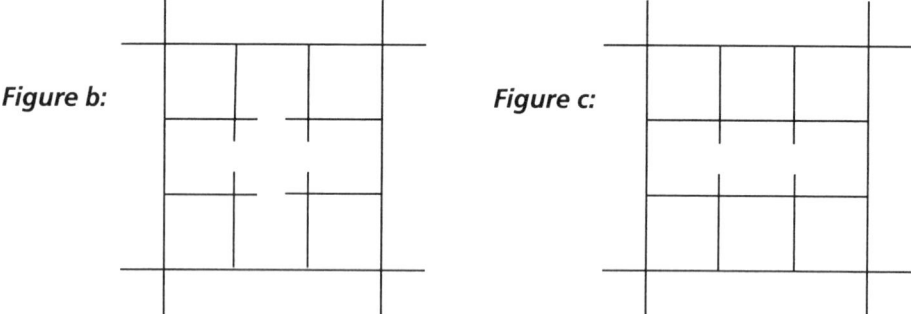

Figure b: *Figure c:*

A review of the impact of the introduction of two hundred 20 mph zones in the UK found reductions in child pedestrian accidents by 70 per cent, child cyclist accidents by 48 per cent, and overall accidents by around 60 per cent. There was a 6.2 per cent reduction in accidents for each one mph reduction in vehicle speed (Transport Research Laboratory, 1996).

On the continent, 10 mph and 20 mph limits have been widely adopted on residential roads, but 4 mph is the limit now favoured in Wohnstrasse developments in Germany. In the UK, the organisation 'Fair Play for Children' advocates an 8 mph limit on residential roads, and it would seem that the pressure to reduce speeds on residential roads from the 20 mph currently favoured by government is very likely to increase (Davis, 1996 personal communication).

❑ The provision of play space

Playgrounds and play areas have traditionally been provided by leisure services or recreation departments, or as an integral part of housing estates by developers or estate owners and managers.

Those provided by leisure services or recreation departments tend to be located in parks, playing fields and other public open spaces. These public open spaces may be quite small pockets of land within or on the edge of housing estates.

In housing estates, playgrounds and play areas have usually been designed into the development plan, or included when the area has been re-developed or renovated. The housing cost yardstick allowance, planning gain, and Urban Programme funding have all been used in the past to fund such provision.

The majority of play areas on council or private estates are handed over to the leisure services or recreation department to maintain them. Occasionally some local circumstances determine that a different department has responsibility for a playground (e.g. education, or social services). In rural areas, parish councils often have responsibility for playgrounds and a small number of playgrounds are run by charitable trusts.

Various difficulties are experienced in the design, location and management of playgrounds and play areas:
- the land used for a playground may be that which is available or left over after the rest has been allocated for houses, shops etc., which may not be in the best location to serve children;
- the person commissioning or designing the playground may have no responsibility for maintenance and there have been numerous instances where playgrounds have been built without any plan for on-going maintenance; and
- although a playground may be designed into a development plan for an estate, it may not be built until after residents have moved in. Consequently people who have got used to a 'nice quiet grassed area' in front of their property often find it difficult to accept and adapt to the impact a children's playground located close to them has.

Generally playgrounds are automatically thought to be the solution to the 'problem' of children's play. There is usually no coherent strategy underpinning development plans to meet the need for children to be able to play throughout an estate, not just at a specific facility.

It is general practice in local authorities to produce Residential Design Guides for potential developers and many have also adopted play policies, sometimes as supplementary planning guidance, which specify a certain level and form of provision (predominantly based on the NPFA *Six Acre Standard*). However, some local authorities have also recognised the value of the total environment for play, not just play areas and require developers to show that the needs of children's play have been considered as an integral part of the whole design process (Sandwell MBC, 1996).

> *All new residential development containing family accommodation will normally be required to provide for children's play at a minimum of 0.8 hectares per 1,000 population.*
>
> *Normally 30 per cent of this should be provided in more formal and/or equipped play space.*
>
> *The balance should be provided in less formal play space and may contribute to wildspace, greenspace, networks etc..*
>
> Draft SPG Policy 1, Sandwell MBC, 1996

Some housing associations such as the William Sutton Trust have also adopted play strategies to guide the provision of mainly formal play facilities for different age groups and the involvement of tenants in the organisation and supervision of children's play on the estates.

It needs to be acknowledged, however, that there is a genuine reluctance for private house builders to formally allocate land for play purposes mainly because of the ensuing, ongoing cost of maintenance of such areas. More commercially acceptable, is the allocation of 'public open space' which can be spread throughout an estate and assessed in a cumulative way. In some cases, this approach has resulted in a smattering of grassed areas in locations which may not be attractive to children but otherwise 'finish off' the layout of an estate from an aesthetic perspective.

The alternative is to offer commuted sums to local authorities to assist in the provision of open space or play areas in the general vicinity of the development. This approach is gradually being resisted by more and more local authorities across the country, who are now preferring to formalise the specific allocation of play areas within new residential estates through the development plan process.

❏ The promotion and supervision of play

There are a number of national 'play' organisations to which people providing for children's play can turn for advice.

These bodies have considerable knowledge and expertise usually on a particular type of facility. Whilst their advice is valuable, and anyone providing facilities would be wise to consult them, they are generally not equipped to talk about children's overall play needs. They are expert in a particular type of facility, believe in the importance of that type of facility and so promote it.

For instance the National Playbus Association will promote the importance of playbuses; Kids Club Network promote the importance of Kids Clubs; and Playlink promotes adventure play. The National Playing Fields Association has traditionally promoted playing fields and children's playgrounds and for a number of years in the 1970s and 1980s promoted adventure playgrounds and holiday playschemes.

This is not to decry the work that these organisations do. The children of this country would be much poorer without them. However, what they do not claim to be are experts in children's informal play away from facilities. The Association for Children's Play (PlayBoard) did try to include this within its umbrella role but this organisation only existed for three years in the mid 1980s. There is currently no national organisation with dedicated staff committed to giving members of the public and local authorities advice on informal children's play, though many of the national organisations mentioned above will give such advice as they are able.

With increasing pressure on local authority budgets, those organisations offering local schemes for children with paid staff (e.g. adventure playgrounds, Kids Clubs and holiday playschemes) are themselves placed under increasing pressure to justify the public finances they receive by giving account of the numbers that attend their facilities. It is not therefore in the interests of these operators to consider or promote children's play needs away from their facilities.

We perceive therefore that there has been a distinct policy shift, since in the 1960s and early 1970s part of the justification for adventure playgrounds was that children could just drop in and out as and when they pleased, and also that the playground enriched the child's experience in things they did outside the playground. It did not matter if the children only stayed for a short time if it stimulated them to do other activities elsewhere. Indeed, part of the role of the playworker was to encourage children not to stay on the playground but to take up other activities.

This shift in emphasis has meant that, whilst many playworkers are sympathetic to children's wider play needs outside their facilities, they cannot see it as a prime concern and may see it as a diversion from their 'real' job.

Notwithstanding the value of the facilities described above it must still be remembered that the majority of children's play, and especially play outdoors on housing estates, is unsupervised and informal.

❑ Play fashions

Children's play activities are influenced by various fashions and crazes and so will alter from time to time. In a previous research project, one of the researchers regularly observed many groups of children playing 'pogs' which was a craze for a short time in the early 1990s. Only one instance of such a game was observed during the current research.

Similarly children's use of wheeled vehicles appears to alter from time to time. Skates, skateboards, roller-blades and carts are all well used by children. During the period of this research in 1996 virtually all the observations of children using wheeled vehicles were on bicycles. If the research had been carried out in another year the picture might be different: roller-blading is clearly a very popular activity in some of the larger urban parks at the moment.

It is our belief that bicycles will always be a high proportion of the wheeled vehicle use. We do not believe that even if we had seen a greater number of other wheeled vehicles on the housing estates, that it would have materially affected our ultimate recommendations. Housing estates need to be designed so that children are able to use bicycles and whichever wheeled vehicle is popular at the time, in an informal way, through the provision of a variety of hard, flat and sloped surfaces.

❏ Involvement

Many people have welcomed the recognition that the Earth Summit in Rio 1992 gave to the fact that environmental problems are inextricably linked to social and economic problems. That these problems belong to all of us and that all of us have to develop a sense of individual responsibility for solving them, requires us to involve every part of society, particularly children, people with disabilities, and those from minority ethnic groups. Much is being made of calls for more 'participation', 'empowerment', 'capacity building' and 'consensus building' that also came out of the Earth Summit in the form of Agenda 21. If these aims are achieved, with growing awareness and participation, children are likely to become more demanding of decent environments and therefore of the professionals who supply those environments.

The recent national conference on Article 31 (children's play) of the UN Convention on the Rights of the Child identified that children's rights to play have been regularly ignored and gave practical recommendations for empowering children to contribute to the development of their own environments.

The Children Act 1989 has recognised the rights of the child to be consulted where they are received to be looked after, however, it was not the intention of this act to address the issue of children's freedom to play. The National Voluntary Council for Children's Play produced a Charter for Children's Play (in 1992) and is encouraging local authorities to adopt its recommendations.

Many local authorities and housing associations are now committed to involving the community in the design of new housing estates or the regeneration of old ones. However, there would seem to be few examples of the involvement of young people, as opposed to adults in such initiatives. Where this is happening, the anecdotal evidence indicates that youth forums, planning for real exercises (where communities construct models of their estates and identify and prioritise the improvements they wish to see), and detached youth worker projects are some of the main vehicles through which involvement is being facilitated.

One of the peculiar difficulties in consulting children is the time scale involved. A community of adults may campaign for, and be involved in the design process of, a community centre over a period of between three and five years before that centre is ever built and occupied.

For a six year old child a three year delay is half a lifetime, and a five year delay is almost a whole lifetime. The needs of a six year old and an eleven year old are significantly different: as are the needs of a nine year old and a fourteen year old. Therefore, time scales from the design to implementation need to be short if particular children are to be involved in ensuring that a specific facility is going to meet their needs. On broader, estate-wide issues, an alternative strategy might be to involve as many age groups as possible to ensure the broadest range of views.

Research Approach

❑ Aims of the research

On the basis of past research outlined in the previous section of the report, a hypothesis was generated that a housing estate which provided good access to a variety of opportunities for children to use would improve both the quality and quantity of their play, and that the value to children living on an estate with such opportunities should be better than that for children living on an estate without.

The main aims of the research were to:

- observe a representative range of housing estates around the country to measure the proportion of children using the outdoor environment, the range of their activities and the relative popularity of different locations within each estate;

- interview children and parents on the estates to widen our understanding of their preferred places for play, their assessment of how good or bad their estate was for play, and their suggestions as to how their estates could be improved;

- identify a variety of processes by which children and young people are being involved in the planning and design or re-design of housing estates; and

- provide a set of guidelines for planners and providers on children's outdoor environmental needs on housing estates and how these might translate into estate design and management.

❏ Research methods: observation and interview surveys

During the school summer holidays of 1996, over 3,500 observations were made of children (under 18 years of age) at play on 12 housing estates built between the 1890s and 1990s, by housing associations, local authorities and private developers (see Table 2: Estate details).

The observers walked around a pre-determined route, noting down each child seen according to their age, sex, basic mode of activity (walking, running, sitting etc.), any key activity (such as imaginative play, active street game etc.) and their location (road, pavement, path, shared surface etc.). Full details of the coding system used are given in the Appendix.

Table 2: Estate details

Date built	Estate type	Number of dwellings
c1900	Inner city terrace	1,000
c1900	Inner city terrace, traffic calmed	700
1920s	Housing association, recently improved	300
1930s	Public, recently improved by housing association	300
1958-60	Public, new town	475
1960s	Public, mixed-rise, recently improved and landscaped	200
1960s	Private, semi-detached, open plan	450
1973	Private, semi-detached	350
1986	Private, semi-detached	425
1990s	Housing association	100
1994	Housing association	150
1994	Private, urban village	300

Observations were made during daylight hours between 9.30 a.m. and 8.00 p.m.. It was noticeable that numbers clearly decreased as the nights grew darker towards the end of the summer holiday period. However, children, and particularly seniors and teenagers, may be outdoors much later at night but our research could not take account of this.

There could be many reasons why children are outdoors apart from the fact that they want to be and are drawn by the opportunities it provides: for example high levels of use of the outdoor environment could be the result of poor indoor environments.

These reasons needed to be explored and so, following the period of observations, 236 children and 82 parents were interviewed using a standard questionnaire format. These interviews were used to draw out qualitative information on:

- the most frequently used locations for play on the estates;
- the most highly valued places;
- unmet needs;
- the constraints on children's play outdoors (access, safety, traffic etc.);
- suggested improvements (access, provision, supervision etc.); and
- parental assessment on whether their estate was a good place for children to play.

In this way we were able to validate why certain places were popular with children (as measured by the observation exercise) and why others were not. It also enabled us to differentiate between 'exciting' places which, though important, may only have been used sporadically, and 'less exciting' places which may have been used for longer periods.

In addition, information has also been gathered from estate managers, local planners and youth workers about their perceptions of where children play on the estates and any problems or particular benefits associated with this.

This method, combining observations and interviews, follows closely that used in the Department of Environment study (DoE, 1973) and deliberately so, to enable the results of this study to be compared with those of the 1973 study. However, it must be made clear that the DoE study focussed on 15 large, relatively modern housing estates, reflecting the thrust of housing policy at that time. In the 1990s, it has been increasingly rare to develop large new public housing estates, and more attention has been given to renewing older stock and creating smaller estates of perhaps 50-300 houses.

It should be remembered that this study was about the design elements of housing estates that facilitate children's play outdoors. Some children's range behaviour enables them to fulfil their outdoor play needs beyond the confines of their estates (especially boys over 10 years of age). It was not possible to investigate this issue in any depth although the interviews generated some qualitative data on it. Equally, we have not looked at the activities organised out of school hours for children at community centres, play centres, or at sports facilities, which also contribute to their play outdoors.

❏ Involving children and young people in the process of change

Whilst the brief required the researchers to examine good practice in the involvement of young people in the planning process, it became obvious that practice is as yet not very well advanced, or not at least, in this country.

Desk research, conferences and personal communications were used to identify the variety of processes that are currently being used to involve young people in shaping their environments, but it has not been possible to find an example where the young people have been involved from the start of the decision making process to the completion or indeed monitoring of a newly built or refurbished estate.

❏ Planning and development issues

The private building industry continues to be in a recession with the need to maximise return from the land by building at high density. Local authority housing departments continue to be constrained and they together with Housing Action Trusts, housing associations and private developers do not always have the expertise to provide relevant opportunities for children's play. There was therefore a need to appreciate the extent to which planners and providers address the needs of children in the design and re-design of housing estates and to examine practical, feasible, low cost ways in which greater access and diversity could be achieved with limited financial resources. Commercial return is and always will be the paramount interest of any private developer.

However, the change in the planning system from a 'development' led system to one of a 'development plan' led system has had a fundamental effect on the way development has and will take place. The power of a local authority to set out clear guidelines on the provision of specific play areas is now more prevalent and more enforceable than ever before. On major schemes, developers are now legally obliged, via Section 106 Agreements, to provide such areas. The key is to make local authorities aware of the fundamental needs of children and for these to be passed on via the planning system to the developer.

The guidelines that have been developed from the results of the study are intended to raise awareness of children's needs. The relevance and feasibility of the guidelines have also been evaluated and refined by planning and housing professionals within the research team and from the Advisory Group for the study.

FINDINGS

The findings from the observations and interviews are presented here and summarised in a table at the end of the section.

❑ Location

■ Playing in the street

It can be seen from a comparison of the DoE's observation findings from 1973 and those of this research that roads and pavements continue to be the most popular location for play outdoors accounting for 46 per cent of all observations (47 per cent if shared surfaces are included) in 1996. There are also more similarities than dissimilarities between the relative popularity of other locations identified in the two studies. So, it would seem that little has changed over the last 25 years.

Table 3: Comparison of the location of play

Location	% JRF 1996	% DoE 1973
Roads/pavements	46	38
Gardens (mainly front)	14	17
Play areas	12	5
Public open space	9	n/a
Grassed areas	9	11
Paths/paved areas	6	24
Other	4	11
	N= 3,605 observations	N= 45,508 observations

In this 1996 study, pedestrian and cycle paths were also popular, where provided, (e.g. 1950s public, new town, and the 1970s – 1990s private and housing association estates) offering children the opportunity to move around these estates more freely without the need to cross roads.

■ To see and be seen

One of the surprising findings of our research was that children spent most of their playing time where they could see and be seen. It might be expected that children would want to play in places where they were hidden away from prying or supervisory adult eyes. This did not appear to be the case. Children were more often seen where they were in open view of houses than they were in areas that were hidden away.

Places that seemed to be interesting places to play, and were hidden away, appeared to be less well used.

Part of the reasons for this were very definite restrictions by parents, for instance, "don't go out of my sight". But children also seemed concerned about what might happen to them in isolated locations. This burden of fear has also been identified in other research (Social Sciences Research Unit, 1996). A feeling of security is therefore also a strong factor in determining where children go.

When they did go further afield it tended to be with other children or with parents, thus maintaining the feeling of security.

Another important factor for children was the desire to be part of the community, "being where it's at". Both the observations and the interviews revealed that children want to be where there is a very strong likelihood that they will meet up with other children or see what's going on. This explains one of the reasons why, in observations, back gardens appear hardly used at all yet front gardens are very popular. In the back garden the child cannot see what is going on, see passers-by or renew acquaintances with friends. In the front garden all these things can happen.

Where children were playing in the front garden they rarely stayed in the garden but used it more as a base from which to run out to greet friends or see what was happening.

Play in back gardens featured as a well favoured location in the interviews, and especially for private, imaginative play, sometimes alone. In the observations however, back gardens were more rarely used. The main exception to this, was on very hot days, when paddling pools were brought out, friends were invited round, and shrieks of fun and laughter were heard from many back gardens and the play there was prolonged. In addition, some young children played in the back garden. However, not all young children were confined to the back garden. Many as young as two and three played in the front garden under parental or sibling supervision.

The back gardens which appeared best used were those at Woodlands, the 1990s housing association estate in York, where wide gaps between the houses, with open fencing, gave visual access for the children in the gardens to whatever was happening in the road outside.

■ Designated play areas

The play areas that were most well used were ones that were open and visible from nearby housing. The children went to and from them on their own. The most popular playground (Broad Meadows, Stafford) was in the heart of a small housing association estate, next to the estate office (affording it some additional informal supervision) and with seats which did appear to encourage some parents to come with their children. The majority of the children there however appeared to be unaccompanied. Public open space and grassed areas accounted for 18 per cent of the locations where children were observed, and play areas 12 per cent.

The exception to this was the play area in a small part at the Chapelfields/Earlsdon area, in inner city Coventry. This was quite popular, but virtually all the children there appeared to be accompanied. The difference between the two areas was that whilst Broad Meadows has short winding roads and culs-de-sac with no through traffic, the Chapelfields/Earlsdon area has long roads with terraced houses through which traffic can pass unhindered. Children were noticeably absent from these roads, neither cycling nor wandering around freely. It would appear that the inner city parents therefore took the children to the play area to compensate for the lack of freedom closer to home.

■ On the move

It would seem that children visit many parts of both their social and physical environment, but do not necessarily stay in one place for very long. Children would be seen calling at a friend's, going into a play area, cycling round but,

Play area for eight year olds located within estate, by estate manager's office with open railings and a seat for adults. Broad Meadows, Stafford.

An informal play area (slide out of view) overlooked on three sides by houses. Woodlands, Stafford.

when the same area was observed half an hour later, there might still be children in that place but not usually the same children.

Where children were observed in one particular place they did not tend to stand or sit still in that place but would break off to greet another child who was going past or to see something else that was happening.

Where there was a group talking it would be quite usual for one or two of the group to be on bicycles and to be cycling round as they were talking.

Whilst children did express preferences for places to play, both in describing their favourite places and what facilities would improve their areas, our observations show that the children did not necessarily spend long periods in these places. This is not to suggest that these places are unimportant for children. Their answers clearly indicate that play areas and parks for instance are very important.

What is important for children is to be able to move freely around their physical and social environment and have a variety of inter-actions at different locations.

This runs contrary to much thinking by both professionals and parents who wish children to have a 'safe place to play'. Even where there was a place that was both safe and popular, they showed no desire to stay there all the time. This finding more than any other highlights the need for developers to design for play throughout the whole of an estate, not just in a segregated (and often isolated) area.

❑ Basic activity

The majority (71 per cent) of all play activity observed was active (see Table 4 for full details).

A comparison with the DoE's 1973 findings indicates that the use of wheeled vehicles has doubled since then, but the level of all other physically active activities has stayed approximately the same.

Most of the seniors and teenagers observed were either walking and talking, or cycling somewhere. Only at the 1950s public, new town and c1900 traffic calmed inner city estates were their needs more fully catered for, to meet and

Table 4: Basic activity observed

Basic mode	%
Walking/running	32
*Wheeled vehicle	20
Standing	18
Play equipment	9
Ball games	9
Sitting	8
Other	4

N= 3,526 observations
* predominantly bicycles, with only a few observations of skate boarding and carting

play ball games on the playing fields and courts of the public open spaces. The additional opportunities to walk and talk along the network of footpaths and cycle tracks, and to fish in a pool in the new town were well used.

❏ Key activity

The most predominant key activity that children were involved in was what we defined as 'going' (Table 5). We found that between 31 per cent and 58 per cent of the observations on every estate were of children who were walking, cycling or occasionally roller skating, purposefully in a definite direction. In addition, 3 per cent to 5 per cent appeared to be on an errand, however, for many observations the destination was uncertain.

Table 5: Key activity observed

Key activity	%
Going somewhere	37
Talking	20
Active street game	10
Imaginative play	6
Other	11
None observed	16

N = 3,131 observations

This finding is crucial to an understanding of how children use their environment. The interviews showed that they have very definite ideas on preferred play places. What is clear is that they travel from one to another, trying them out, and meeting different friends. The travelling to and from, constitutes a significant amount of any time spent outdoors.

The lowest varieties of key activity were observed at the 1994 urban village estate in Harlow (although this might be the effect of a small sample and a new community), the 1960s open plan, private estate in Coventry and the 1990s housing association estate in York.

The highest levels of imaginative play e.g. playing house, schools, and building, occurred at the 1930s public, recently improved by a housing association estate, Moat Farm in Sandwell. This could be as a result of the traditional culture of the estate, the ease of access to a relatively wild, informal open space adjacent to the estate and the lack of formal play facilities forcing the children to invent more of their own activities.

There was a distinct lack of quiet street games such as marbles or pogs, (again with the exception of Moat Farm). Such games do tend to come into fashion and go out again quite quickly which may account for this finding. Alternatively, there could be a deeper, long term trend that the children of the 1990s, though mobile and sociable, show an increasing lack of ability to stay still and concentrate for very long on anything, like the traditional games favoured by the children of the 1970s (DoE, 1973). Where quiet street games were observed they were more often than not being led by an older child emphasising the way in which such play is passed down from generation to generation. These games were played out on front garden walls or on street corners where the pavement widened out to create a space where it was possible for a small group to crouch down away from the kerb edge.

❑ The proportion of children outdoors

Where it has been possible to obtain 1991 census figures on average household size and the percentage of under 16s in the population for estates, the proportion of children observed at play outdoors has been calculated (Table 6).

Table 6: Proportion of children outdoors

Estate	% Children outdoors
1930s public, recently improved by housing association	24
1950s public, new town	22
1994 housing association	20
1980s private	15
c1900s inner city, traffic calmed	9
c1900s inner city	8

These percentages are comparable to those observed in the DoE 1973 study where never more than 20 per cent of resident children were observed to be out of doors. Of more significance perhaps are the differences between estate types. As might have been expected, there is a much lower proportion of children outdoors on the inner city terrace estates as compared to the estates with a greater amount of accessible outdoor space close to homes and formal play provision located within safe and short walking distances from home.

The 1980s private estate, whilst built on a cul-de-sac layout with a footpath network, housed families with, on average, older children than the housing association estates. The attractions of computers and other indoor activities for the older age groups might therefore account for the proportion outdoors being slightly lower than might have been expected.

These figures emphasise the contribution designing for diversity and accessibility can have on children's play and therefore on their physical, mental and social development.

❑ Age group and gender differences

The relative proportion of males to females is closer than might have been expected (67 per cent to 33 per cent) given what we know about the restrictions on the range of girls below 10 years of age (Matthews, 1987). However, this was a study confined to investigating children's play relatively close to home and this might account for the closer ratio. Alternatively it may be that girls are becoming more liberated in their use of the outdoor environment, as evidenced in the rise of girls' football and rugby. A ratio of 71 per cent to 29 per cent, males to females, was recorded by Millward (1989) in open spaces.

Table 7: Gender differences

Estate type	% females	% males
c1900 inner city, terrace, traffic calmed	23	77
c1900 inner city	44	56
1920s housing association	44	56
1930s public, recently improved by housing association	41	59
1950s public, new town	33	67
1960s public, mixed rise, recently improved and landscaped	33	67
1960s private, open plan	45	55
1970s private, semi-detached	34	66
1980s private, semis/detached	37	63
1990s housing association	43	57
1994 private, urban village	41	59
1994 housing association	39	61

❏ Favourite places to play

When asked for their regular and favourite play places children consistently referred to green open spaces (park, fields) and, if there was one available locally, an equipped play area (Table 8). If there was a single tree or a small copse of trees then these were also very popular and particularly so for climbing. These three types of location stand out well above all other locations as the regular or favourite places children say they use. The frequency of reference to these places in the interviews far exceeds the observed behaviour of the children where the majority of play was recorded as taking place in the front street.

Findings

Change of surface, tight turn into culs-de-sac and off road parking within culs-de-sac. Broad Meadows, Stafford.

Tree for climbing in view of passers by, grassy area, footpath link, off road parking. New Earswick, York.

Table 8: Regular and favourite locations reported

Locations	%
Open space (park and grassy area, field)	56
Street/road	23
Play area	21
Friends	19
Tree	17
Back garden	16
Outside house	16
Shops	14
Front garden	7
Other	13
Total	*202

N = 236 children
* % total is greater than 100 because some children gave more than one answer

The most frequent activities referred to in the interviews (Table 9) were football and cycling, closely followed by use of playground equipment, playing in trees, and other active games.

Table 9: Activities reported at favourite and regular play locations

Activity	%
Football	33
Bikes	28
Friends	24
Play equipment	19
Trees	11
Hanging around	8
Other	9
Total	*132

N = 236 children
* % total is greater than 100 because some children gave more than one answer

The most significant reason quoted for going to a particular place was 'friends', i.e. meeting up with and playing with (Table 10). This was closely followed by parental permission, proximity to home, and 'space'. Answers were allocated to 'space' when children talked about it being a 'big area', or 'there's room to…'. Where there were trees available these also formed a substantial reason for using a particular place: to climb, swing from or meet under.

Table 10: Reasons for liking favourite and regular play locations

Reason	%
Friends	27
Play equipment	21
Space	18
Approved of by parents	14
Trees	13
Good for active games	12
Safe	9
Can do what you want there	8
Animals	8
Can ride bike	6
Sports equipment (e.g. goal posts)	6
Other	32
Total	*** 174**

N = 236 children
* % total is greater than 100 because some children gave more than one answer.

Going to, or being able to be with 'friends' appears high up the ratings as a preferred place to play, a key activity and a reason for liking favourite or regular play locations (see Tables 8, 9 and 10).

Children are keen to be sociable and need spaces within sight of home and within a couple of streets from home where they can meet each other and play.

❑ Parental perceptions

The main reasons parents gave for their estate being judged good or bad for children related to the presence or lack of facilities (55 per cent) and busy or quiet roads (27 per cent). Safety or danger was only mentioned by 22 per cent and was much lower than might be expected particularly when danger included all references to bullying, older teenagers, and drunks. This was also reflected in the reasons given by parents for restricting children's ranges: roads (29 per cent), bullying, 'stranger danger' and drunks (10 per cent).

Parents frequently asserted that their children had to stay within eyesight of home (46 per cent). Within hearing and shouting distance accounted for a further 9 per cent of mentions, and round the block or within a couple of roads 29 per cent. It was clear from the observations that children were travelling some distance away from home beyond that approved by parents, but then not that much further. Although the majority would appear to travel beyond eyesight, they still remained within one or two roads from home on most of the estates.

Whilst children's ranges do increase with age, there still appears to be a strong desire, both for security and convenience, to stay relatively close to the home. Many of the parents with teenage children still expressed strong reservations about their children going far away from the home.

❑ Suggested improvements

The suggestions children put forward largely related to amenities already present on their estate or in their locality, but not necessarily accessible to them; perhaps because they were in a dangerous state of repair or required an adult to accompany them. The suggestions included the need for more play areas, youth or after school clubs, sports centres, parks and traffic calming measures.

We have taken the view that the improvements children desire need to be assessed in the light of observed behaviour and their stated preferences for locations and activities. They also need to be related to the existing availability and accessibility of such locations and activities within each estate.

Accessibility includes the feeling of security and being part of the community. If these two criteria are not met then even if an opportunity appears to be available, it may still not be accessible for many children. For example, when a small clump of trees was located within eyesight of homes, then it was well used. Larger groups of trees, out of eyesight were less well used. The same effect was observed for play areas sited within and on the edge of estates.

This approach overcomes the difficulty of children's limited ability to request improvements in estate design or outdoor facilities that are beyond their experience. For example, a child who has never played in a cul-de-sac is unlikely to suggest it as an improvement for their estate.

❑ Layout

The layout of the estates recording the highest proportion of children outdoors could be stylised as culs-de-sac off a loop road, but with even less linkage to the loop and main road system than suggested by DB32 (see Figure d).

Figure d:

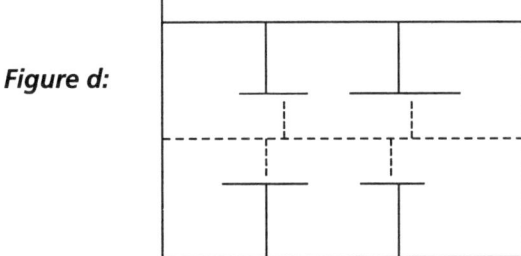

What is just as critical for children is the accessibility of a footpath network, which ideally links into open spaces and play areas, within and adjacent to the estate. These conditions have been met in the case of the layouts for the 1950s public new town, the 1994 private, urban village, the 1990s housing association estates, and the 1973 and 1980s private estates. The option for children to be able to walk or cycle round the block along a path and pavement network and so be able to access grassy areas, parks and open spaces without the need to cross main roads was appreciated by the children and their parents. With this option children have the opportunity to extend their ranges and therefore potentially experience a larger and more diverse outdoor environment.

There is a need to change our way of thinking. Our aim should be to provide a safe and interesting environment for play, not just a safe place to play.

In contrast, to access the public open spaces in the inner city estates required children to either cross busy main roads or to travel across too many long straight roads to get to them (see Figures e and f).

The traffic calming measures that had been introduced at the 1930s public estate would seem to have created a perception of relative safety in the minds of parents and children alike. Signs reminding motorists that they were entering a 20 mph zone, changes in surfacing material, humps and closed off roads, all helped to slow traffic down even on the long straight roads, at least during the day. Parents reported some joyriding activity in the evenings. Off street parking and low front garden walls on which the children frequently played also helped to increase the visibility of children playing in the street for motorists.

A summary of the findings for each estate is provided on pages 49-51.

❑ Supervised play

None of the estates studied had full-time supervised play facilities within them. However, there was voluntary involvement with the play area at one of the 1990s housing association estates, some part-time playwork within the park at one of the inner city estates and some part-time playwork at the 1990s urban village. Whilst it is not the duty of those building housing estates to provide playworkers, it is important for them to consider that these might be provided in the future. Discussions with the appropriate local authority department(s) may reveal whether or not there is a possibility of full or part-time or voluntary playwork schemes being provided. By considering this possibility at an early stage, appropriate provision might be made, e.g. toilets, storage within existing or planned public buildings, or open space so designed that, should funding become available, the opportunity would exist for a community building or play centre to be erected.

Figure e: Estate layouts

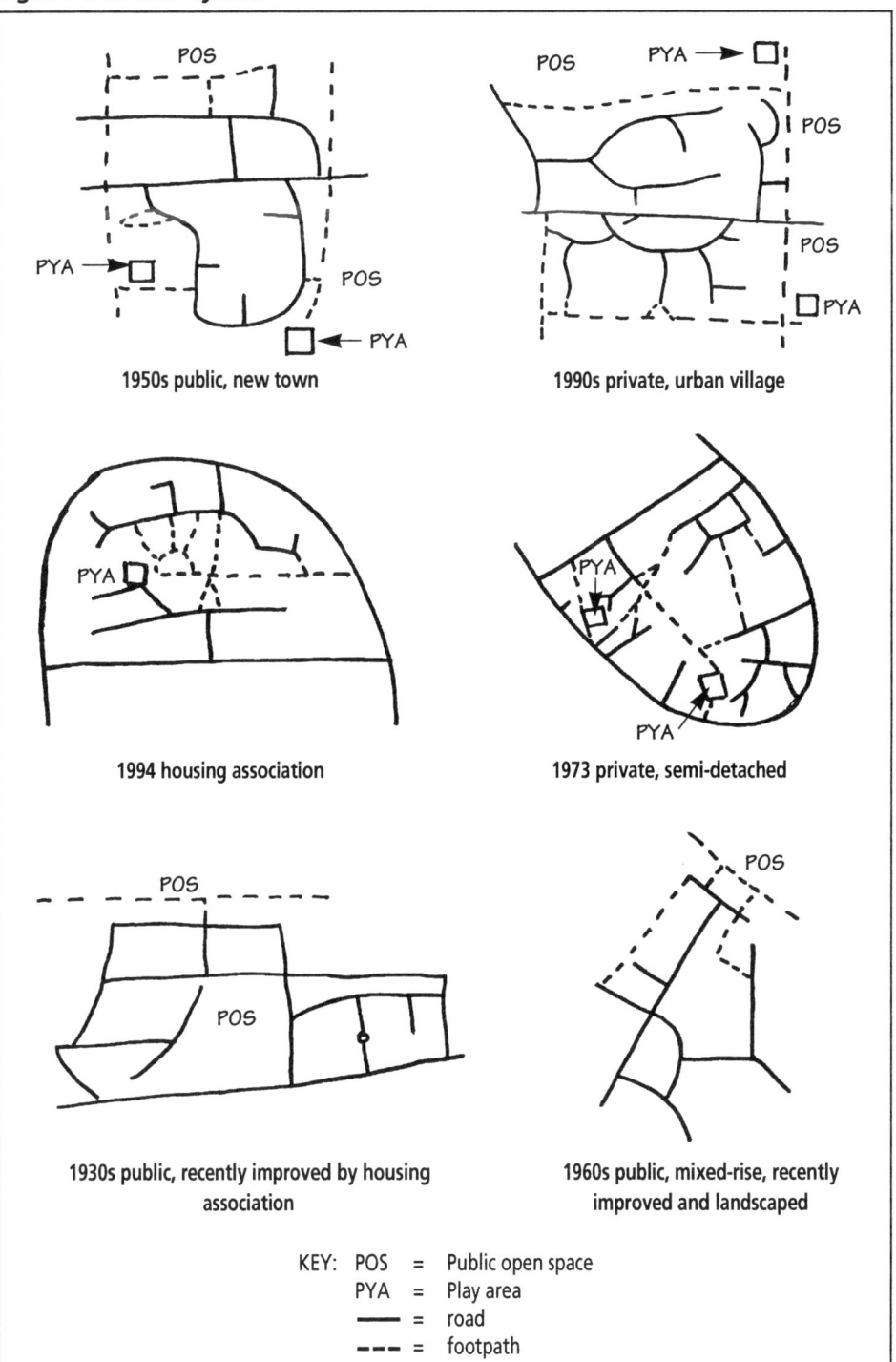

Figure f: Estate layouts

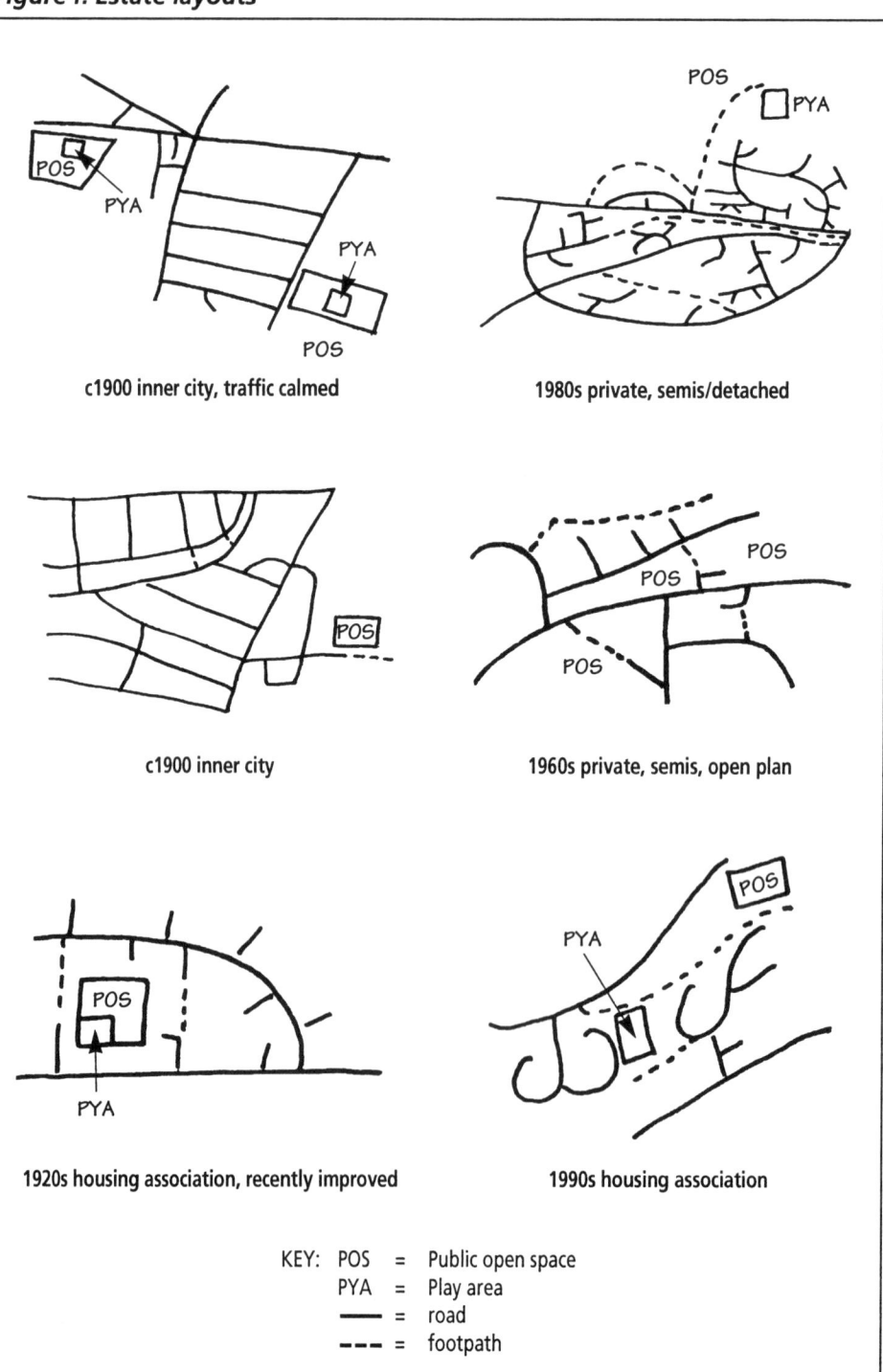

❏ Summary of findings on each estate

The summary of findings indicates how each estate performed in terms of the level and range of basic and key activities, the location of play activity and parental assessment.

Estate type	Factor	Findings
pre 1900 inner city, terrace	location	use of play area high; roads and pavements low
	basic mode	use of play equipment high, wheeled vehicles low
	key activity	low levels of imaginative play and active street games
	parental assessment	bad
1900 inner city, terrace, traffic calmed	location	use of parks and play areas high
	basic mode	use of wheeled vehicles low; ball games high
	key activity	level of active street games high
	parental assessment	good
1920s housing association	location	use of public open space high
	basic mode	level of standing, sitting and ball games high; wheeled vehicles low
	key activity	level of going and active street games high
	parental assessment	mixed
1930s public, recently improved by housing association	location	use of roads/pavement and front gardens high no play area on estate
	basic mode	levels of standing and wheeled vehicle use high
	key activity	levels of imaginative play and quiet street games high
	parental assessment	mixed
1950s public, new town	location	use of paths, public open space, play areas high; roads and pavements lowest
	basic mode	level of sitting, standing and ball games high
	key activity	level of going and fishing high
	parental assessment	mixed

Estate type	Factor	Findings
1960s public, mixed rise, recently improved and landscaped	location	use of roads/pavement and informal public open space high; grassed courtyards low
	basic mode	walking/running and use of wheeled vehicles high
	key activity	levels of going and imaginative play high
	parental assessment	bad
1960s private, semis, open plan	location	no play area
	basic mode	level of standing high; ball games low
	key activity	level of active street games low
	parental assessment	mixed
1973 private, semi/detached	location	use of paths high; roads/pavements low
	basic mode	ball games high; wheeled vehicle use highest
	key activity	active street games high; going average
	parental assessment	good
1980s private, semis/detached	location	use of roads/pavement, public open space and play area within, high
	basic mode	use of wheeled vehicles, standing and play equipment high
	key activity	level of active street games highest; imaginative play lowest
	parental assessment	very good
1990s housing association	location	use of play area in park high
	basic mode	use of wheeled vehicle high
	key activity	level of imaginative play low
	parental assessment	mixed

Estate type	Factor	Findings
1994 private, urban village	location	use of roads/pavement, shared surface and play area high
	basic mode	use of wheeled vehicles high
	key activity	level of going high
	parental assessment	mixed
1994 housing association	location	use of paths and play area high; road/pavements low
	basic mode	use of play area highest
	key activity	use of play equipment highest; going and imaginative play average
	parental assessment	mixed

❏ Conclusions

There is a need to change our way of thinking. Our aim should be to provide a safe and interesting environment for play, not just a safe place to play.

The conclusions to be drawn from the research show how children make use of the outdoor environment of housing estates beyond that of play areas. Children's needs are multifarious: places for physically active play and quiet games; places which encourage social contact; and places which allow them to be mobile on foot and by bike.

■ Location

- children still use the front street most for play;
- estates which stimulate the highest level of outdoor play are those with the greatest variety of places and the slowest traffic; and
- estates which stimulate the widest range of play activity and satisfaction amongst children and parents are those with footpath networks, culs-de-sac layout, public open spaces and play areas.

■ Activities

- the majority of play is physically active and nearly always involves moving around the estate;
- moving around the estate to be with friends is a main activity; and
- children like to see and be seen.

■ Preferences

- children strongly desire access to play areas, parks and trees; and
- seniors and teenagers are not well catered for and desire access to footpath networks, sports pitches and courts, and pools for fishing.

■ Layout

- the front street is the most frequently used location for outdoor play;
- for children to exploit this environment fully, traffic speed needs to be reduced to 10 mph and as much of the road and pavement as possible needs to be visible to motorists and pedestrians within residential roads;
- children's mobility and therefore their access to as large an outdoor environment as possible is optimised by the incorporation of a footpath network, and a culs-de-sac layout;
- play areas are best located along the footpath network, within public open spaces, adjacent to public buildings or well used pedestrian routes that afford a degree of informal community supervision; and
- parks and open spaces are best located along the footpath network or adjacent to well used pedestrian routes.

Children's needs for safe access to a diverse outdoor environment on the front street and opportunities for extending their free range mobility along footpath networks and traffic calmed roads, need to be incorporated in the estate design and management process.

WHOSE ESTATE IS IT ANYWAY?

INVOLVING YOUNG CLIENTS IN THE PLANNING AND DESIGN PROCESS

In the course of gathering data for this research, we have met and talked to over 200 children many of whom have been able to describe the problems they experience in using the outdoor environment of their estates and their ideas as to how things could be improved. We have asserted that the views of children, restricted though they may be by definition, as a result of their limited life experience, ought to be taken into account in the design or re-design process, in combination with what we know about their actual behaviour outdoors and the accessibility of opportunities.

However, whilst there would seem to be a number of initiatives underway in various parts of the country to involve children in estate design or regeneration, a consensus on the most successful techniques or processes has yet to emerge. Instead, there is a growing awareness and willingness, mainly within the local authority and housing association sectors to try out a variety of techniques with different groups of young people. These techniques all of which have been or could be adapted to designing new or refurbishing existing estates, include:

- planning for real;
- youth forums;
- detached youth worker projects; and
- surveys and presentations.

Planning for real exercises involve people in constructing a home made model of their estate or neighbourhood, in order to be able to move elements around and prioritise in a very visual way what needs preserving, demolishing or changing. The process can be facilitated by an impartial non-resident, a planner, youth worker or teacher. The Neighbourhood Initiatives Foundation (which developed the technique) can provide do-it-yourself packs.

Youth forums have been established by some urban regeneration initiatives such as City Challenge and Local Agenda 21. They often have a broad remit to look at young people's needs in an area including employment, leisure and training. Their links to formal planning and implementation agencies could be better exploited if new ways and less intimidating ways could be found to debate and make decisions other than through adult dominated committees. There are over 30 youth forums covering whole towns in the UK and many of these are supported by a number of smaller forums at a neighbourhood or ward level.

Detached youth workers, with a brief to work with young people who do not belong to traditional youth organisations on estates, can facilitate the involvement of young people in defining needs and developing proposals and funding bids, to bring about change. These workers should be able to link in with planning and regeneration agencies to represent or negotiate representation of their clients' views.

Surveys and presentations can be carried out by any informal or formal group of young people. Schools are becoming increasingly interested in looking for real life examples of planning issues which can be used for project work within the national curriculum. These techniques can be particularly valuable with older age children as they can learn skills in carrying out the surveys and presentations. And, as it is the senior and teenage age groups that seem to be least well provided for on estates, identifying the needs of these groups and the preferred locations for new facilities can be most useful in defining which adult communities may need to be influenced.

Some examples of actual initiatives which have involved or could involve young people are described below. Not all the examples relate to single estate-based projects, and it is therefore necessary to interpret how the principles involved in the examples could be applied to single estate initiatives. What comes out of the experience of these initiatives is the difficulty of:

- ensuring that a degree of co-operation and mutual support is generated between the young people's initiative and the estate planning or management agency; and
- ensuring that there are practical opportunities for young people to act on decisions made for change, e.g. building construction, landscaping, decorating, organising festivals, fund raising, running playschemes, and the like.

The examples cover the who, what, where, when and why plus any outcome, of processes where young people have been involved in housing estate design or regeneration.

Allerton and Lower Grange Young People's Project, Bradford

A detached youth worker works with young people on the estate who do not go to youth groups or school to develop projects using principles of social action.

The youth worker is responsible for managing the process of involvement and the young people are responsible for the content.

The principles of social action promoted by the youth worker are:
- the need to respect the views, skills, understanding and ability of all stakeholders we work with;
- that people have a right to be heard and a right to choose whether or not to become involved in defining issues and taking action on them;
- to acknowledge the complexity of causes and solutions to problems;
- that people who lack power as individuals can gain it by working together in groups;
- that workers facilitate and do not lead the process; and
- to challenge all forms of oppression whether by reason of age, race, gender, sexual orientation, class, disability or any other form of social differentiation.

Despite efforts by the Urban Regeneration Authority to talk to and involve young people on the Allerton Estate, the young people became alienated. The professionals wanted the young people's committee to be entitled 'Young People and Crime' and the young people did not find it easy to contribute to the predominantly adult committees overseeing the regeneration process.

With the detached youth worker, the young people carried out a survey of their peers of what they liked, disliked and felt should be improved on the estate. A need for more single person flats and a cafe were identified.

A video was made of the survey and a successful bid for £300,000 was made to the National Lottery by the young people to put towards the construction of a drop-in centre on the estate.

Tipton Youth Forum

Tipton Youth Forum was set up in 1993 to ensure that young people had an input into the decisions made during the life of the City Challenge urban regeneration initiative in this part of the West Midlands.

There are 12 primary schools and 2 secondary schools in Tipton and the initial group of 11-25 year olds (brought together by youth workers in the area to start the forum) went into the schools to explain what the forum was and how representatives would be elected to it.

Following the presentations, brainstorming sessions were held, a newsletter was launched and a database was created of interested young people and their ideas for the area. Once again the main need seemed to be for a drop-in centre.

More children voted in the election of their representatives to the youth forum than did their adult counterparts in the local government elections.

The young people here have had significant support from the youth service in setting up the forum, organising events, and undertaking a school survey.

The youth workers have been appreciated as:
- always there;
- positive, enthusiastic, motivating;
- showing us our options; and
- suggesting (but do not dictating) directions.

It has been more difficult to contribute to the planning process within City Challenge. The young people have felt:
- intimidated by the adult dominated committees and the jargon heavy language;
- that they are not always listened to or taken seriously;
- that one young person on each committee cannot represent all young people; and
- the timing of meetings in, or at the end of, business hours often precludes them from attending if they are still at college or at work.

These young people have involved thousands of local people in events they have organised, made direct contact with several hundred young people in their area, been signatories to a Single Regeneration Budget bid, raised tens of thousands of pounds, run the forum budget and generated a number of jobs.

Translating this model to that for the design or re-design of an estate would suggest:
- identifying a handful of keen and relatively able teenagers to get things going;
- organising a survey of children's needs through the local school(s);
- setting up a youth forum through elections and then electing two representatives to sit on relevant estate committees;
- providing access to training opportunities on running meetings, presentation skills, negotiating, fund raising, planning and business management; and
- providing training for adults working on committees with these young people to ensure they support the young people's involvement.

Children and neighbourhoods in London

In this five year programme, run by the Children's Society, around 1,000 five to nineteen year olds will be asked for their views on a yearly basis on everything from graffiti and re-cycling equipment to playgrounds and youth facilities.

A youth worker from the Children's Society has also been appointed to encourage youth clubs and community centres to come forward with their ideas on the failure of estates, public transport, and dog-free reserves.

This initiative will be run across five local authority areas, Lewisham, Hackney, Camden, Bexley and Enfield.

Support is also being provided by Planning Aid for London.

A Guide for Teachers and Planners, RTPI West Midlands Branch

The West Midlands Branch of the Royal Town Planning Institute has published a guide for teachers and planners on involving young people in planning issues. The guide has already been distributed to every secondary school in England and Wales but is also suitable for primary school children.

There is guidance on how planning issues can be used to help deliver the National Curriculum and various appendices give information on the planning process, departmental and professional roles.

The publication would be useful to youth workers and estate managers in areas which are to undergo re-generation or where the building of a new retail development could generate community benefits for say open space or play equipment.

Advice is given on:

- selecting a planning issue of relevance to young people or the locality of their school;
- analysing why an issue is an issue, e.g. type, location, scale of development, environmental, social and economic impact;
- key questions to ask;
- learning strategies or activities, e.g. interviews, desk top research, role play, surveys, presentations; and
- sources of professional help, e.g. local councillors, planners, nature conservationists and economic development officers.

What all these examples show is that:

Children and young people can clearly do much to identify their own needs, plan for change, raise the funds and provide practical effort to improve their estates and neighbourhoods. The real challenge is for those of us who stand at the gates to welcome them in. Identifying someone on the design team to act as a mentor for the young people and liaise with the youth service would be a major step forward.

We would be grateful to learn of more examples of children and young people's involvement in estate design and management initiatives.

GUIDELINES

The main findings of the research have been used to generate a set of guidelines for architects, planners and estate managers. The guidelines are structured as a set of objectives which providers may wish to consider for the design or regeneration process, linked to practical measures that can be taken to achieve those objectives.

The ideal estate would be designed so that children would be able to move freely throughout the neighbourhood, able to enjoy a wide variety of social interactions and opportunities for physical, imaginative and creative play.

Objective	Measure
1. To enable children to move freely round their estate on foot, bicycle, skates, or other wheeled vehicle.	• Footpath network linked to grassy areas, tarmaced areas, play areas, school, shops and bus routes.
2. To travel safely without danger from traffic.	• Traffic calming measures to limit car speeds to 10 mph: short straight sections, bumps, culs-de-sac, change in surface material or colour, roundels, pinch points, mini-roundabouts and sleeping policemen. • Culs-de-sac and no through route layout. • Narrow sight lines on approach roads and sharp angle turns into residential roads. • Wide sight lines to enable drivers to see children moving between pavement and road within residential roads. • Car parking off road, on drives or in bays to increase visibility of children moving between pavement and road.

Objective	Measure
3. To be able to play in front, or within sight, of their homes.	• A variety of play spaces and surfaces incorporated in the front street landscape, such as walls, sitting areas, grassy areas, and sections of wider pavement, to encourage girls especially to play outdoors, as they tend to have more restrictions placed on them than boys. • Front gardens with good visual oversight from house kitchens and living rooms. • Footpath network linked to grassy areas, tarmaced areas, play areas, school, shops and bus routes.
4. To be part of the community and the community's interactions.	• A variety of play spaces and surfaces incorporated in the front street landscape, such as walls, sitting areas, grassy areas and sections of wider pavement, to encourage girls especially to play outdoors, as they tend to have more restrictions placed on them than boys. • Public open spaces located along popular pedestrian routes to shopping centres, schools and other well used public buildings such as estate offices, to increase the level of informal community supervision.
5. To be able to play in the natural environment.	• Trees and hedgerows conserved and incorporated as street landscape features to encourage climbing and imaginative play. • Public open spaces incorporating play equipment (with swings and a slide as a minimum), trees, wild areas and flat grassy areas for ball games.
6. To be able to play in purposefully provided play opportunities.	• Play areas located along footpath network, within public open space, adjacent to public buildings or well used pedestrian routes, to allow for a level of informal community supervision. • A variety of play spaces and surfaces incorporated in the front street landscape, such as walls, sitting areas, grassy areas, and sections of wider pavement, to encourage girls especially to play outdoors, as they tend to have more restrictions placed on them than boys.
7. To be able to play football and other ball games.	• Public open spaces incorporating play equipment (with swings and a slide as a minimum), trees, wild areas and flat grassy areas for ball games. • For seniors and teenagers, a footpath network, flat surfaces for sporting activity, laid out pitches and courts, a fishing pool and places to meet, in public open spaces, within or adjacent to estates.

Objective	Measure
8. To be able to play outdoors within the home environment.	• Back gardens with sections of fence or gate which allow children to see what is going on in the street. • Front gardens with good visual oversight from kitchens and living rooms.
9. To be able to attend playschemes, clubs or other organised activities.	• Facilities designed or useable for playwork, either paid or voluntary, regular or occasional. • Play areas located along footpath network, within public open space, adjacent to public buildings or well used pedestrian routes, to allow for a level of informal community supervision.

These guidelines have also been used to produce a checklist which follows. Using it, architects, planners and estate managers can assess the quality of provision for children's needs for the outdoor environment on proposed and existing estates.

CHECKLIST FOR PLANNERS AND ESTATE MANAGERS

The checklist on the next pages can be used by planners, architects and estate managers to judge the extent to which an estate (proposed or existing) meets children's needs from the outdoor environment close to home. A simple tick and cross method of scoring can be used to provide a quick assessment of a design or layout.

Feature	Present
Variety of surfaces on each street:	
walls	
front gardens	
wide pavement in places (for quiet street games)	
trees for climbing	
grassy areas	
hedgerows	
Layout:	
culs-de-sac	
no through route layout	
short straight road sections (60 metres)	
winding roads giving short sight distances ahead	
traffic calming measures on long straight roads (change of surface, pinch points, mini-roundabouts and sleeping policemen)	
back gardens with sections of fence or gate which allow children to see what is going on on the street	
front gardens with good visual oversight from kitchens and living rooms	
Footpath network:	
footpath network for pedestrians and cyclists to allow for round the block mobility without the need to cross roads	
spinal layout	
links to: − schools − shops − bus routes − play areas	
Safety:	
off road parking	
wide sight lines within residential roads	
community supervision	

Checklist for Planners and Estate Managers

Play areas:	
adjacent to footpath network	
within public open space	
beside public building	
beside well used pedestrian route (e.g. to shops, school, bus route)	
central location for each catchment	
seating for adults to encourage informal supervision	
equipment for under eights	
equipment for over eights	
Facilities for teenagers:	
football pitch with wooden goal posts	
courts	
informal open space for meeting places (tree clumps, grass, benches)	
public open space	
footpath network	
fishing pool	
Wild areas:	
trees	
hedgerows	
shrubberies	
other	
Water:	
paddling pool (supervised)	
paddling pool (unsupervised)	
pond or stream in public open space	
pond or stream in wild area	
ephemeral feature (e.g. path that puddles in wet weather)	

❑ Supervision

Supervision of play areas is considered desirable especially for school holiday periods and particularly for play areas which incorporate paddling pools or other water-based amenities. If an estate is being built in an area where such supervision is provided, the needs of a play or leisure officer (e.g. storage space, toilet and first aid facilities) need to be designed in.

❑ Crime and safety considerations

The guidelines are a direct response to the findings of the study and therefore very much reflect the users' perspective. However, some of the measures suggested need to be carefully planned and designed, to reduce the likelihood of them facilitating crime on some estates.

Planning out Crime (Circular 5/94) sets out government policy on design and crime prevention practice while the Home Office Crime Prevention Centre is constantly updating its guidance and policy on the same matter. Reference to this information should be made when considering design for children's needs.

The following points should be taken account of:

1. Culs-de-sac with no through route layouts linked into footpath networks can provide 'escape routes' which are very difficult for police in vehicles to police.

   Culs-de-sac should be discrete areas which theoretically will only attract vehicles to the properties they serve thereby keeping traffic generation to a minimum.

2. Although it is important to allow pedestrian and cyclists direct access to play areas, access for emergency vehicles should still be included.

3. As research by the emergency services has found, the design of traffic calming measures varies. In the worst cases, such measures restrict the free flow of emergency vehicles to an unacceptable level. However, it needs to be remembered that the need for emergency vehicle access could be reduced if more people were able to gain the health benefits of

convenient and safe access to the outdoor environment of estates for their physical recreation.

Any traffic calming design must therefore be very carefully prepared and discussed with all the relevant parties before implementation.

4. The guidance in DB32 on narrow width sightlines for approach roads should be followed. But, developers should be encouraged to allow for wider sight lines wherever possible within residential roads.

5. Trees, hedgerows and other vegetation should not be planted close to entrances to alleyways or the like, where individuals could use it for ambush. Nor should it be planted close to buildings where it could facilitate entry to upper floors.

   Furthermore, if vegetation and trees are to be incorporated, these areas should not only be able to resist 'rough treatment' but should also be easy to maintain.

6. Providing walls and the like as part of the general street furniture, i.e. which do not form a boundary function and would therefore not be under the control of a householder, could be beneficial.

   However, what can be upsetting for householders is the congregation of what may appear to be 'gangs' at particular locations and the vandalism of private property, such as low walls at the end of a garden fronting onto the street.

   This emphasises the need for some organisational structure through which children's needs can be addressed and conflicts mediated, on estates; be it a residents' or tenants' association, a youth project or something else.

7. A footpath network linking culs-de-sac to grassy areas, parks and play areas, whilst ideal for children, also makes it much easier for criminals to escape from being chased by police vehicles. This problem can be reduced by making some of the path corridors wide enough to take a vehicle and ensuring that all paths ultimately link to a loop road so that the criminal must come out of the estate at some point beside a main road. Community surveillance is also an important factor in deterring crime on estates, and it could be argued that the more children there are out at play on an estate, the more adults are keeping an eye on them and so too the general street scene. Effective community supervision is

achieved through the development of this sense of territorial 'ownership' of the communal areas close to people's homes and is essential for the safety and welfare of children.

It has to be remembered that children can account for up to 50 per cent of the residents on some estates and the outdoor environment outside their homes is the most frequently used place for physical and social play.

Society must make the decision as to whose needs are paramount: the adult residents who may still have the opportunity to fulfil their play and development needs elsewhere, or the children who cannot?

APPENDIX

❑ JRF: Observation coding system

A. **Age**

		Code
Pre-school	0-3	P
Infant child	4-7	I
Junior child	8-11	J
Senior child	12-14	S
Teenager	15-18	T
Subgroup: Disabled		Dis

B. **Sex**

	Code
Male	M
Female	F

C. **Activities**

Basic Mode	Code	Key Activities	Code
Walking or running	W/R	Imaginative play	imp
Ball games	BA	Talking	t
Wheeled vehicles	WV	Picnicking	p
Play equipment	PE	Reading	r
Sitting	SI	Observing wildlife	ow
Standing	ST	Vandalising	v
Lying	LY	Harassing	h
Paddling	PA	Going	g
Climbing	CL	Running errand	e
		Gymnastics	gy
		Quiet street game	qsg
		Active street game	asg
		Watching others	wo
		Walking dog	wd
		Fishing	f

D.	Location	Code
Roads, pavements, garage courts	R/P
Paths (Paved areas)	PT (PVA)
Shared surface	SS
Garden Front/Back	GDF/B
Access areas	AA
Grassed areas	GA
Planted areas	PLA
Play areas	PYA
Wild areas	WA
Unorthodox areas (tops of walls, roofs, building site)	UNO
Public Open Space	POS
Unknown	U

BIBLIOGRAPHY

AKEHURST, A. and WHEWAY, R. 1982. *Talking About Play*. Humberside Playing Fields Association, Goole, National Playing Fields Association.

ALLIED DUNBAR. 1992. *Allied Dunbar National Fitness Survey*. London, Health Education Authority and Sports Council.

van ANDEL, J. 1990. Places Children Like, Dislike, and Fear. *Children's Environments Quarterly* 7 (5): 24-31.

ANDERSON, J. and TINDAL, M. 1972. The Concept of Home Range: new data for the study of environmental behaviour. In *Proceedings of the Environmental Design Research Association*. Los Angeles, UCLA.

ARMSTRONG, N. and McMANUS, A. 1994. Children's fitness and physical activity among 11-16 year old British Children. *British Medical Journal* 301, 28 July: 203-205.

BERNALDEZ, F.G., AIELLO, R.P. AND GALLARDO, D. 1985. Environmental Challenge and Environmental Preference: Age and sex effects. *Journal of Environmental Management* 28 (1): 53-70.

BIRMINGHAM CITY COUNCIL (1997). *A Nature Conservation Strategy for Birmingham*. Birmingham City Council.

BJORKILD-CHU, P. 1977. Children's Outdoor Environment. Summary in: *Man-Environment Systems*. July/September: 250-251.

BOX, J. and HARRISON, C. 1993. Natural Spaces in Urban Places. *Town and Country Planning*, September: 231-235.

BRADLEY, C and MILLWARD, A.M. 1986. Successful Urban Greenspace – do we know it when we see it? *Landscape Research* 11 (2): 2-8.

BUSSARD, E. 1974. *Children's Spatial Behaviour in and around a Moderate Density Housing Development: an Exploratory Study of Patterns and Influences*. M A thesis (Unpublished) Cornell University.

CALE, L. and ALMOND, L. 1992. Physical activity levels of young children: a review of the evidence. *Health Education Journal* 51(2): 94-99.

CHARTERED SOCIETY OF PHYSIOTHERAPY. 1995. *Physiotherapists concerned about unfit, fat, flabby young people*. Press release, 26th June.

COATES, G. and BUSSARD, E. 1974. Patterns of Children's Spatial Behaviour in a Moderate Density Housing Development. In Carson, D. (Ed) *Man-Environment Interactions*. 12, Milwaukee: EDRA.

COFFIN, G. and WILLIAMS, M. 1989. *Children's Outdoor Play in the Built Environment*. London, The National Children's Play and Recreation Unit.

COOPER MARCUS, C. 1974. Children's Play Behaviour in a Low-Rise Inner City Housing Development. In Moore, R.C. (Ed) *Childhood City* Vol 12. Environment Des. Res. Association 5: 197-211.

COULSON, N. 1980. Space Around the Home. *Architects Journal* 172(52): 1245-1260.

DATTNER, R. 1969. *Design for Play*. Rheinhold, Van Nostrand.

DAVIS, A. and JONES, L. 1996. The Children's Enclosure. *Town and Country Planning*. September: 233-234.

DEPARTMENT OF THE ENVIRONMENT. 1961. *Homes for today and tomorrow*. London, HMSO.

DEPARTMENT OF THE ENVIRONMENT. 1973. Children at Play. *Design Bulletin* 27. London, HMSO.

DEPARTMENT OF THE ENVIRONMENT and DEPARTMENT OF TRANSPORT. 1992. Residential Roads and Footpaths : Layout Considerations. *Design Bulletin* 32. London, HMSO. Second Edition.

DEPARTMENT OF THE ENVIRONMENT. (Forthcoming). *Handbook of Estate Improvement. Part 2 External Areas*. London, HMSO.

DEPARTMENT OF TRANSPORT. 1995. *National Travel Survey 1992/94*. London, HMSO.

ELLIS, M. J. 1973. *Why people play*. Prentice-Hall Inc.

ESSEX COUNTY COUNCIL. 1973. *A Design Guide for Residential Areas*. Essex, Essex County Council.

GUMP, P., SCHOGGEN, P. and REDL, F. 1963. The Behaviour of the Same Child in Different Milieux. In Barber R.G. (Ed) *The Stream of Behaviour*. New York, Appleton-Century-Crofts.

HARSHA, D. 1995. The benefits of physical activity in childhood. *American Journal of Medical Sciences* 310, supplement 1:S109-113.

HART, R. 1979. *Children's Experience of Place*. New York, Irvington.

HILLMAN, M. 1988. Foul Play for Children: a price of mobility. *Town and Country Planning* 56 (12).

HILLMAN, M., ADAMS, J. and WHITELEGG, N. 1990. *One false move: A study of children's independent mobility*. London, Policy Studies Institute.

HOLE, V. 1966. *Children's play on housing estates*. London, HMSO.

HOLME, A. and MASSIE, P. 1970. *Children's Play: A Study of Needs and Opportunities*, Michael Joseph.

INSTITUTE OF EDUCATION. 1996. *Children, Parents and Risk*. Social Science Research Unit, University of London.

JENDREK, M.P. 1988. Outdoor Recreational Needs Assessments: The importance of drawing 2. *Journal of Leisure Research*.

KARN, V. and SHERIDAN, L. (1996). *Housing Quality. A practical guide for tenants and their representatives*. York, Joseph Rowntree Foundation.

KEGERREIS, S. 1993. Independent mobility and child mental and emotional development. In Hillman, M. *Children, transport and the quality of life*. London, Policy Studies Institute.

KUHL, D. and COOPER, C. 1992. Physical activity at 36 years: patterns and childhood predictors in a longitudinal study. *Journal of Epidemiology and Community Health* 46:114-119.

LONDON PLANNING ADVISORY COMMITTEE (LPAC). 1992. *Open Space Planning in London*. Romford, LPAC.

MATTHEWS, M.H. 1987. Gender, Home Range and Cognition. *Trans. Inst. Brit. Geogs. New Series* 12: 43-56.

MATTHEWS, M.H. 1992. *Making Sense of Place: Children's understanding of large-scale environments*. Hemel Hempstead, Harvester, Wheatsheaf.

MCLELLAN, J. 1968. *The Question of Play*. Pergamon.

MILLWARD, A.M. 1987. *Community Involvement in Urban Nature Conservation*. PhD thesis (unpublished). Birmingham, Aston University.

MILLWARD, A.M. 1989. *Children, Nature and the City: A Research Study into Children's Experience of Nature Through Play Outdoors*. Birmingham, (Unpublished).

MILLWARD, A.M. and MOSTYN, B.J. 1988. *People and Nature in Cities*. Peterborough, Nature Conservancy Council.

MOORE, R. 1986. *Childhood's Domain*. London, Croom Helm.

MOORE, R. and YOUNG, D. 1978. Childhood Outdoors: Toward a Social Ecology of Landscape. In Children and the Environment, Vol 3, *Human Behaviour and Environment*. (Eds) Altman, I. and Wohlwill, N.F. New York, Plenum: 83-130.

NATIONAL PLAYING FIELDS ASSOCIATION. 1992. *The Six Acre Standard: Minimum Standards for Outdoor Playing Space*. London, NPFA.

NAYLOR, H. 1983. Children's Playgrounds: an observational study. *Play Times* 39: 8-9.

NAYLOR, H. 1985. Outdoor Play and Play Equipment. *Early Child Development and Care* 19 (1): 109-130.

NOSCHIS, J. 1992. Child development theory and planning for neighbourhood play. *Children's Environments* 9(2): 3-9.

OWENS, P.E. 1988. Cultural Landscapes, Gathering Places and Prospect Refuges: Characteristics of outdoor places valued by teens. *Children's Environments Quarterly* 5 (2): 17-24.

PARKINSON, C.E. 1985. *Where Children Play*. Association for Children's Play and Recreation and Carrick James Market Research. Birmingham, PlayBoard.

PIAGET, J. 1951. *Play Dreams and Imitation in Childhood*. Heinemann.

RAITAKARI, O., PORKKA, K., TAIMELA, S., Rasanen, L. and Vikari, J. 1994. Effects of persistent physical activity and inactivity on coronary risk factors in children and young adults. *American Journal of Epidemiology* 140(3):195-205.

RHODE, C.L.E. and KENDLE, A.D. 1994. *Human Well Being, Natural Landscapes and Wildlife in Urban Areas*. Peterborough, English Nature.

SLEAP, M. and WARBURTON, P. 1993. Are primary school children gaining heart health benefits from their journey to school? *Child: care, health and development* 19(2): 99-108.

SLOMAN, L. Streets for People. *Town and Country Planning*. 1996, July/August: 194-195.

TITMAN, W. 1994. *Special Places Special People*. Winchester, Learning Through Landscapes Trust.

TRANSPORT RESEARCH LABORATORY. 1996. *Review of Traffic Calming Schemes in 20 mph Zones*. Report 215. Crowthorne,TRL.

WHEWAY, R. 1995. *Streets for all children and for the total child*. Paper to 'Play in the Streets Conference', London.

WINTER, J., COOMBES, T. and FARTHING, S. 1993. Satisfaction with space around the home on large private sector estates: lessons from surveys in Southern England and South Wales, 1985-1989. *Town Planning Review* 64(1): 65-88.